WHO AM I?

Jean Klein, a musicologist and doctor from Central Europe, spent his early years inquiring about the essence of life. He had the inner conviction that there was a 'principle' independent of all society and felt the urge to explore this conviction.

His exploration led him to India where he was introduced through a 'direct approach' to the non-mental dimension of life. Through living in this complete openness, he was taken, one timeless moment, by a sudden, clear awakening in his real nature. It was not a mystical experience, a new state, but the continuum in life, the non-state in light of which birth, death and all experience take place.

From 1960 he led a quiet life teaching in Europe and later in the United States.

WHO AM I?

THE SACRED QUEST

Jean Klein

Compiled and edited by
Emma Edwards

NON-DUALITY PRESS

Jean Klein Foundation
PO Box 22045
Santa Barbara, CA 93120
United States

jkftmp@aol.com
http://www.jean klein.org

Cover illustration: Frau in der Morgensonne
by Casper David Friedrich

Non-Duality Press is an Imprint of

newharbingerpublications, inc.
5674 Shattuck Avenue • Oakland CA 94609 • USA
800-748-6273 • fax 510-652-5472
www.newharbinger.com

ISBN: 978-0-9551762-6-5
www.newharbinger.com

ACKNOWLEDGEMENTS

I would like to express my gratitude to Mary Dresser
and Henry Swift for all their help in preparing this
publication, and to Pat and Barbara Patterson for their
many useful suggestions.

CONTENTS

PREFACE

This book came to life through dialogues which took place in different countries with people from all walks of life, and especially through stimulating conversations I had with Emma Edwards. These often touched the border of the inexpressible. I deeply thank her for writing down what cannot easily be written, the nearest formulation to what is beyond words, so that the mind of the reader may be enlivened and clarified. Only a clear mind dares to give itself up to its Origin, that which has been and ever will be.

In writing this some sentences from Plato's *Letters* come to mind:

I certainly have composed no work in regard to it, nor shall I ever do so in future, for there is no way of putting it in words like other studies. Acquaintance with it must come rather after a long period of attendance on instruction in the subject itself and of close companionship, when suddenly, like a blaze kindled by a leaping spark, it is generated in the soul and at once becomes self-sustaining.

Jean Klein

INTRODUCTION

The desire to question life comes from life itself,
from that part of life which is still hidden.
Life provokes us to question. It wants to be admired.
As long as it is not, the question remains.

The question Who am I? appears so often in our lifetime
but we turn away from it. There are many moments in
which we are provoked to ask, What is life? Who am I?
Perhaps we have felt, since childhood, a vague nostalgia
for 'more', a divine longing. Perhaps we feel that the real
reason for our birth is eluding us, passing us by. Maybe
we have become bored with all the ways we have used
to try to give meaning to our existence: the accumulation
of learning, experiences and wealth, religious pursuits,
compulsive busyness, drugs and so on. Or we are facing a crisis in which we no longer feel we can control
the situation. Perhaps we simply dread death. All these
happenings are opportunities that should not be wasted.
They come from life itself, calling us to look, because
life knows that when we really see it, we cannot help
but admire...

Why do we avoid the call to inquire? Why do we
avoid discovering what we are? Largely because there
is the deep feeling that to inquire earnestly means the
death of something we hold onto, this something being
the idea we have of ourselves, the personality, the ego
and all that comes with it. But we also hesitate because
we really do not know how to ask the question, we feel
it there but cannot approach it, we feel it too big for us,
we are in awe of it. The wonder of it is that both these

excuses belong to our inherent wisdom, come from the answer itself. They prove that we already know more than we think.

The first step in self-inquiry is therefore to see what cowards we are, how we avoid every opportunity to really inquire, how we shun the yearning or the feeling of lack. We may acknowledge them intellectually but we don't really welcome them. As soon as we admit this reaction, we will feel life provoking us to inquire at every moment. The question is always there underlying all our compensatory activities.

Once we have accepted life's challenge we need to know how to ask the question so that it has power, can be effective and not disappoint us. We must become convinced that the question will take us to the answer. Our questioning must become worthy.

To come to effective self-inquiry we have to be clear about how it differs from other kinds of inquiry. Our everyday questions naturally assume that the answers will mean something to us, that they will relate to our experience, our memory. These questions presume a centre of reference, an 'I' who can compare and interpret. The assumption of an answer on the level of the question is perfectly valid in the world of reference where comparison and memory are essential tools. This is how we communicate verbally. But when we ask Who am I? we are questioning this centre of reference, questioning the questioner, and obviously what is in question cannot give an answer. In this arena of inquiry memory has no role, for what is there to compare to 'I' or Life? We cannot step out of them. We are they. So we are brought to a stop with nowhere to go. We just don't know. It is possible to spend a lifetime hovering here at the limits of concept where Kant found himself, but where for the philosopher is the end of inquiry, for the truth seeker is just the beginning. For this is the moment when one moves from spiritual inquiry led by a forefeeling of the answer to what could be called the sacred quest, which is the answer.

The real quest begins when this not-knowing ceases to be an agnostic concept and becomes a living experience. This occurs suddenly when the stopping of the mind's efforts is actually felt on every level, that is, when it becomes an immediate perception rather than merely a cognition. When the 'I don't know' state is accepted as a fact, all the energy which hitherto was directed 'outside' in its search for an answer, or 'inside' in its search for interpretation, is now released from projection and is conserved. In other words, attention is no longer directed to the objective aspect but returns to rest in its organic multi-dimensionality. This is manifested as a sudden orientation, a shift in the axis of one's existence, *the end of looking for answers outside the question itself.* Allowing the not-knowing to be fully explored takes the inquirer into a new realm. It is a new way of living. It is a state of expansion on every level, an openness to the unknown and thus to the all-possible.

There is nothing introverted or mystical about living in openness, in non-directed alertness. The tools of existence, memory and the 'I', come and go as needed but the presence in which they come and go remains. The disappearance of the centre of reference no longer means unconsciousness, a blank, a death. There is the continuum of consciousness, Life, in which all phenomena appear and disappear. Only in this is there absolute security and fulfilment. From now on the residues of formulation, of subjectivity become more economical, fuelled by nothing outside the question itself until the residues of the Living Question are dissolved in the Living Answer.

WHO AM I?

The following pages are gathered from public talks
and private conversations with Jean Klein in Europe and
the United States. They have been loosely grouped so
that different aspects can be emphasized and explored
in depth, but the principle remains the same throughout.
This principle is not an idea, not a synthesis of opposites,
not a kind of monism – all of which are concepts. Nor
is it a state of any kind, a mystical feeling of union, an
ecstasy, a negation of the world. Rather it is the timeless
non-state in which all states arise and dissolve. It is the
continuum in activity and non-activity. It is Life itself,
our natural being. In this book different words such as
consciousness, beauty, wholeness, silence, ultimate subject, god, global awareness, meditation, home-ground,
background, stillness, truth and so on, are all names in
different verbal contexts for the same all-encompassing
living principle. Once the principle has been seen, the
reader must not hesitate or remain passive, but experiment in transposing it into all areas of life. The real
content of such words is living understanding. The real
poem comes after the reading.

E.E.

PROLOGUE

Q. What can you give me?
A. Being here is giving.

Q. What is given?
A. What you ask for.

Q. What am I asking for?
A. Remember what brought you here, the motive.

Q. Curiosity.
A. You appear too serious to have come simply from curiosity, as you might go to a circus. Before you formulated your motive, what was there? Perhaps a feeling of lacking something?

Q. Maybe. But a lack of what?
A. Of being related. It was loneliness that brought you here. The origin of all lack is feeling isolated.

Q. Yes . . . it's true. If I'm quite frank with myself I must admit I often feel isolated. I can't understand it, because I have so many friends.
A. You are no longer nourished from the whole. You take yourself to be an individual. You cannot live in autocracy.

Q. How can I become nourished by the whole, as you say?
A. You are the whole. See only that you think you are a fraction.

Q. If taking myself for an individual has become a reflex what can I do about that?
A. Simply note the mechanism. In seeing it you are already out of it. It may continue for a while but it is no longer fuelled by your involvement. This mechanism is in you but you are not in it. At the moment of seeing it, the reflex is no longer emphasised. So when you see it clearly, it reveals you as the seer.

Q. In looking at something there is already a space-relation, isn't there? I can't really see something I'm right inside.
A. Exactly. Take note that you know yourself only in constant producing, in memory. You do this for the survival of the I-image. Come to a stopping of all projecting and abide in receptive alertness. It is a passive-active state. In moments free from producing there are spontaneous appearings. These you will eventually recognise as your being, wholeness, your presence. First you recognise stillness, then you are it. You feel yourself as autonomous, that is, not identified with what is all around you. And now true relation is possible.

RELATIONSHIP

Is there relation in oneness?

To be human is to be related. As a human being we live in relation with the elements, the sun, moon, the stones in the earth and all living beings. But what does 'to be related', 'to live in relation with' mean? Generally, when we use the word we mean a link of some kind between individual entities, object to object, or subject to object. The word relationship here presupposes separateness, the joining together of fractions. This fractional view of relatedness is purely conceptual. It is a figment of the mind and has nothing to do with pure perception, reality, with what actually is.

When we live free from all ideas and projections, we come into real contact with our surroundings. Practically speaking, therefore, before we can be related to our environment we must first know how to be related to that most near to us, body, senses and mind. The only hindrance to the clear perception of our natural state is the forceful idea of being a separate individual, living in a world with other separate beings. We have an image of ourselves.

This image can be maintained only in relation to things and thus it makes objects of our surroundings, friends, children, spouse, intelligence, bank account, etc., and enters into what it calls a personal relationship with these projections. The fanciful idea of a self is a contraction, a limitation of wholeness, real being. When this notion dies we find our natural expansion, stillness,

19

globality without periphery or centre, outside or inside. Without the notion of an individual there is no sensation of separateness and we feel a oneness with all things. We feel the surroundings as occurrences in unrestricted wholeness. When our lover or children leave home or our bank account drops, it is an event *in* us. Awareness remains constant.

All phenomena, all existence is an expression within globality and the varieties of expression only have meaning and relationship in light of the whole. To be related is to be related within the whole. Since there is no meeting of fractions, in the whole there is no other. Strictly speaking, therefore, in perfect relation there is no relationship, no duality; there is only globality. All perception points directly to our primal being, to stillness, the natural non-state which is common to all existence. Thus, in the human expression, to be related is to be in communion with the whole. In this communion the so-called other's presence is felt as a spontaneous giving and our own presence is a spontaneous receiving. There is no longer a feeling of lack and consequently a need to demand, because simply receiving brings us to our openness. When we live in openness the first impulse is offering. Being in openness and the spontaneous movement of offering is love. Love is meditation. It is a new dimension in living.

Q. You say there is no other but you cannot possibly say that there are no differences between people. I have my character and capacities just as others have theirs.

A. You live in contraction, thinking of yourself as an individual. Where do the terms 'me' and 'mine' find meaning? When you really look into yourself you cannot say the body belongs to you. You are the result of two people and each parent had two parents and so on. All humanity is in you. You are what you absorb. You eat vegetables, fish, meat, and these are dependent on light, the sun, warmth. The light is related to the moon and the stars are all related. There is nothing personal in us. The body is in organic relationship with the universe. It is made of the same elements as everything else. The composition of the elements varies but this variation is almost negligible in human beings. There may be differences in structure and colour but the constitution and functioning are the same in all of us. There is nothing personal in the heart, liver, kidneys, the eyes, ears or skin, nor in the elements which build patterns of behaviour, thinking, reactions, anger, jealousy, competition, comparison, and so on. These are the same emotional states. The body-mind functions in a universal way and the care that has to be taken is the same in all.

You must understand and co-operate with the body. It is ignorance of the mechanism that creates conflict. Inquiry can only be carried out in daily life. Your mind and body are reflected in your behaviour from morning until night. Your attention must be bipolar, observing the inner and outer fields. Relationships are the mirror in which your inner being gets reflected. Be aware that you are a link in the chain of being. When you really feel this, the emphasis is no longer on being individual, and spontaneously you come out of your restriction. You do not live in isolation, in autonomy. In relatedness is the fore-feeling of presence.

Q. So the individual does not exist as an isolated entity. But does not the personality exist as a unique part of the whole?

A. The person is really only persona, mask, but it has come to be synonymous with the idea of an individual, separate and continuous entity. The personality is not the constant we imagine it to be. In reality it is only a temporary reorchestration of all our senses, imagination and intelligence, according to each situation. There is no repetition in life and each reorchestration is unique and original like the design in a kaleidoscope. The mistake is to identify with the personality, to conceptualise it in memory and then take ourselves for this collection of crystallised images rather than letting all emotions, perceptions and thoughts arise and die in us. We are in the theatre watching our own play on stage. The actor is always 'behind' his persona. He seems to be completely lost in suffering, in being a hero, a lover, a rascal, but all these appearings take place in global presence. This presence is not a detached attitude, a witnessing position. It is not a feeling of separateness, of being 'outside'. It is the presence of wholeness, love, out of which all comes. When no situation calls for activity we remain in emptiness of activity, in this presence.

Q. When you are no longer identified with the person, how is life affected?
A. The first thing you notice is how much richer and deeper your perceptions are. Communication becomes so much more varied. Generally, we are fixed in patterns of communication but when we live in openness a great sensitivity arises, a sensitivity we never dreamed of.

When we approach our surroundings from wholeness our whole structure comes alive. We do not hear music with the ears only. When the ears cease to grasp sound for themselves we feel music with our whole body, the colour, the form, the vibration. It no longer belongs to a specific organ. It belongs to our whole being. This creates a deep humility, an innocence. Only in humility is true communication possible.

Then one lives in a completely new dimension. To live as a personality is to live in restriction. Don't live in restriction! Let the personality live in you. In living in the environment without separation there is great, great beauty.

Q. Would you talk more about humility in human relations?

A. Humility is not something you wear like a garment. It has nothing to do with bowed heads and averted eyes! It comes from the reabsorption of individuality in being, in stillness. It comes from the ending of all agitation. In attention, alertness, there is humility. It is receptivity, openness, to all that life brings. Where there is no psychological memory, no accumulation of knowledge, there is innocence. Innocence is humility.

In intimate or problematic situations, each must speak in humility of how they feel. It is simply a statement of facts with no justification, no interpretation. We must not look for a conclusion. If we allow the situation complete freedom from evaluation and judgement and pressure to find a conclusion, many things appear which do not belong to our memory.

Humility arises when there is no reference to an 'I'. This emptiness is the healing factor in any situation. Heidegger says, 'Be open to the openness.' Be open to non-concluding. In this openness the situation offers its own solution, and in openness we receive it. Often when the solution appears the mind comes in and quarrels with it, doubts it.

Q. Is offering, love, present even when someone is being extremely negative?

A. Because you are always receptive, everything appears as a gift and points to your real nature. It is not what points that is important but the receiving attitude. In receptivity all objects unfold and are transmuted into love.

When someone is being negative and you do not provide a hold for his negativity, he may suddenly be brought back to himself. It is as if he reaches out to grasp a door handle he is sure is there and, finding it not there, suddenly becomes aware of his empty hand. Then the situation no longer belongs to an image. It belongs to observation itself.

Q. What is the basis for our choice of friends before we reach the point of being ego-free?
A. You can't look for friends. They come to you. The background of all meeting is the moment when there is nothing to say. Here there is feeling without emotivity. If this background is not present in a lively way you can be sure it is only covered by words, projection and images. A man or woman does not exist in him – or her – self. They appear in this background occasionally. It is only in this absence of expectation that the qualities of man and woman can appear without clichés and repetitions. Generally, between two people, there is very little real meeting. There is only the coming together of two patterns. This causes conflict and boredom.

Your neighbours and friends have ideas about you. Do not be taken in by these ideas or in turn have ideas about them. Don't imprison people in your memory. Circumstances never repeat; life never repeats. It is only the ego which desires a known security that labels every being and situation. So live in your surroundings as if for the first time. Be without qualifications. In this nakedness you are beautiful and every moment is full of life.

Q. How can I know when I am being impulsive and when spontaneous?

A. Impulsive behaviour is reaction. It is conditioning. When you take yourself for nothing you are a loving being and there is no reaction. What you say or do belongs to the situation itself and not to an idea. Spontaneous action is free from memory. It is perfectly aesthetic, beautiful and right. It is fundamentally ethical.

Q. More specifically, I am not clear about when sexual desire is compulsive or impulsive and when it is a spontaneous expression of love.

A. In true love there is no lover or beloved. There is a moment which comes from the body to celebrate that love on the bodily plane. This oneness in body sensation springs directly from the oneness of love itself.

The behaviour between two lovers is an art. An artist appeals to his highest imagination. But imagination must be used to exalt love not to compensate for its lack. Biological rhythm and imagination are carried by love and it is only love that can constantly renew stimulation; otherwise, there is boredom.

Today, unfortunately, there is great confusion about what is desire which flows from biological rhythm, and desire which comes from the mind and is mechanical repetition. There is so much mental stimulation that most people have lost touch with their biological rhythms and have become dulled or mechanically greedy. Mechanical repetition hinders natural rhythm. In mechanical repetition there is only taking and using. When the mind, memory, intervenes, the body is no longer open in all its capacities and then sensual stimulation is no longer powerful and you compensate with images and effort. It is a vicious circle.

You must be clear about the nature of your desire.

Do not let second-hand information influence you. There is only love and in this love the man and woman sometimes appear. There is no habit, no automatic reflex in this appearing. Most so-called responses to people are just habits and reactions.

Q. Is there such a thing as immoral behaviour?
A. When you live as consciousness, every moment brings morality which springs out of beauty. For those who live in beauty, codified morality is immoral because what may be moral in the situation today may not be appropriate for tomorrow. Codified morality accepts repetition. When every moment brings its own moral understanding and way of acting, there is an interior plasticity of mind and body. As long as you call yourself a personal identity you are motivated by security and compensation and there is no adequate living in the moment. This is the condition of people today. We live in a lame society where there is no ripeness and no maturity. That is why, in a certain way, codified morality prevents the society from crumbling completely. So when we give our children codified behaviour as a crutch, it must be with the firm conviction that one day they will be able to act intelligently.

Q. You said the behaviour between lovers is an art. Does this mean all sexual expression is aesthetic?
A. When all appears in love and disappears in love, is an expression of love, why live in restriction? There is no man or woman present, there is only love. This unconditioned love may be transposed onto the biological level but what is called sexuality does not exist for me. When there is only a biological act or some temporary sentiment there is often a feeling of losing something afterwards. This creates a psychological reaction of aversion or indifference of which you may not be aware. You

may only be aware that you have lost interest in each other. In a relationship based primarily on biology there is separateness. But the moment the biological function is an extension of living in oneness there is no feeling of separation. The joy of oneness is true love and will never lose its attraction.

In the expression of love, all is moral. You are a poet, an artist, a musician. You celebrate with your whole being.

Q. It seems that when I live from moment to moment it inevitably brings intimacy in many relationships, with no comparison and nothing really problematic. I seem to fall in love quite easily and I have always assumed that this is just my nature.

A. You are living for the moment but not in it. You are still completely identified with the different images on the film, still living in becoming, in experiences and adventures. What you call 'falling in love' is attachment to a state. There is no real emotion in it, no thing new. It is security for the image of yourself as a man or a lover. Why restrict yourself to an image? See that the light which illuminates the film is not itself coloured.

In relationships of one personality to another, one image to another, there is only conformity, exploitation and demanding. There is compulsion and violence. In supreme intimacy there is sensitivity and a great sense of beauty and elegance. Body relationship is a crowning physical manifestation of the togetherness of a spiritual state. But for the body relation to be elevated to such heights it must come as a spontaneous outflowing between two lovers living really in oneness.

Q. But I feel harmonious with many people and there is a natural call in me to actualise this on the physical plane. I can move from one love to another with complete ease.

A. Your body has been misused and has become completely conditioned. This behaviour is a mental pattern in which selective discrimination has been systematically repressed. Without this pattern the body is completely free and mature sensitivity arises in which selective discrimination comes to play.

Q. So when you say that love is not exclusive it has nothing to do with intimate relationships?
A. Love belongs to all. You don't need to confirm it on a physical plane with all.

Q. You said earlier that real friendship is the silence when there is nothing left to say. Would you talk more about this?
A. Let us say you live with someone you really love. There may be many moments when there is nothing to feel and nothing to think. There is only being together. You often feel it with couples who have been together a long time. When you live with a man or a woman there comes a time when you know all about each other's past and there is nothing left to say. But the intervals are full, not empty, and the complete comfort in the interval is the background of the whole relationship. Then it is beautiful to be together. Everything comes out of this silence and dissolves back into it.

Q. As a parent is there any way to bring up children not to be identified with the personality?
A. Until a certain age the child looks constantly through you to appropriate himself in the world. So you must be free and it is your freedom that is the teaching. How the parents behave is very important. There are so many

things that cannot be said but only demonstrated in living. Of course there is authority in your way of behaving but it is not an imposed authority. Real authority is never authoritarian. It comes from impersonal wisdom, not the personality.

The child must understand that there is no repetition. One must never fix an experience. He must always be inquiring. Every event should be faced in a new way. This means that you do not face your child as something definite, a child, but at every moment face his totality. Never compare him with another. If you take yourself as a parent and your child as a child, he feels himself imprisoned though he may not know why he feels this way. There must be friendship between parent and child. In friendship there is no father, no mother and no child. There is only love.

Q. How can I educate my child so that there is no repetition?
A. Where there is imagination there is no repetition. Until the age of 7 or 8 the right brain should be emphasised. This is the feeling, global sensation, intuitive part. The child should remain in painting, playing, music, dancing, and so on. The analytical left brain can be developed later with this as a background.

Q. What about sending children to schools?
A. Our educational system is primarily built up for the survival of the person. There is very little humanity in our education. All is structured around psychological survival in a society built on competition. But young people are the beginning of a new society. If you educate the child at home, he has the opportunity to become a beautiful being, but you must face such a responsibility intelligently and with open eyes or he may turn around

when he is older and accuse you of not providing the tools for surviving in the world as it is now!

Q. How can I bring up a child to know that codified behaviour is only a transition?
A. You must be free from codified behaviour yourself. Never bring restrictions to a situation. Of course, the situation may bring its own restrictions functionally and morally. But these restrictions don't come from an idea. They come from your whole seeing, from total intelligence.

A child first learns this from his family nucleus. When there is right feeling, doing and thinking in the parents, the child spontaneously imitates right behaviour.

Q. I find I worry a lot about money. Is this justified?
A. You are not the owner of what you have. You are the administrator. When you are an administrator and not an owner you'll behave completely differently because you are free from it. You will utilise it differently according to the situation and not with a view to accumulation. Spend money graciously!

Q. How can we know how much we need? I have a family and tend to worry about the future.
A. When you come to know yourself you come to a hierarchy of value. As you no longer emphasise the phenomenal, you use the world completely differently. Don't associate yourself with a competitive, productive society that constantly creates needs, new elements for survival. Our society is bound to consumerism. It's a completely artificial creation.

Don't spend too much time working for money to accumulate! You should be able to work three or four days a week or have half the day to live in beauty. When you have a family the present has a certain extension. How far it goes only you know, but don't live in the future!

Q. We spoke earlier about how to face anger when it is psychological reaction, an emotional state. Can anger ever be reaction-free?
A. Yes. There is a divine anger but then it is not really anger. It is a kind of activity that is unrelated to any self-image. It is the upcoming of the totality in a gesture of the rightness of function. From outside it may look like anger but it is not anger. It is completely free from reaction and leaves no residue. The moment the situation is over it completely dissolves.

Q. Can this impersonal action ever be involved in fighting?
A. The moment one's biological environment, that is, body, family, cow and shelter, are in danger, spontaneous action arises. It springs from the desire to protect, from biological survival which is free from fractional viewpoints and the idea of an 'I', to maintain.

Action is therefore completely integrated in a global view and is appropriate to the moment. It does not outlast the situation but dissolves back into stillness, wholeness, from which it arose.

Q. What about action in large-scale war?
A. Collective anticipation is always psychological, the defence of ideas. A society which never acts in anticipation, on idea, will never be aggressive. The way to behave in war depends on the moment itself. There must be dignity in defence. Reaction-free action springs from intelligence. We have focused on only one way of solving conflict – physical annihilation. But conflict can be

resolved in any number of ways. One cannot say beforehand which way is suitable. When you live free from
egotistical motivation your capacities are surprisingly
varied!

Q. So there may be times when it is right to fight with
passive means?
A. One acts according to the moment free from prede-
termined psychological and political ideas. Then there is
presence to the situation and only in this presence can
intelligence function. To have an ideal of passivism in
all situations is no more intelligent than to have an ideal
of aggression. All means must be at your disposal. You
cannot be fettered by ideals. There may be times when
inviting your aggressor into your house and giving him a
meal is right acting. But there is no such thing as passivism. There is only acting. Non-acting is also acting.

Q. What do you think of nationalism?
A. Biological survival includes the community, language,
rituals, customs, and so on. Culture is an extension of
the individual, so in a sense the deep urge to protect the
culture is part of biological survival. But nationalism is
based on idealism. It is an abstraction, a fabrication. It is
collective psychological survival. The protective instinct
of biological survival has a certain limit, the limit of
physical security. It is impossible that biological survival
alone could lead to grand-scale war. The limits of psychological survival, on the other hand, are less defined.
Psychological survival stems from the mind and will go
as far as the mind goes.

Q. You say that we must be free of ideals. What do you
see as the function of idealism?

A. It is a tool of society to organise the various individuals and small groupings of individuals which naturally make up a culture into a larger and more homogeneous collectivity. All idealism, even the most spiritual, is based on calculative thinking and becoming. War of course belongs to the becoming process, to comparison and aspiration. It is becoming for the hypothetical survival of the person, when, in fact, there is no person.

Ideals may take you to war but at the moment of fighting where are the ideals?

Q. How can I best bring about peace in the world?
A. So you're looking for peace? You'd like to see your surroundings in peace? Are you in peace? Because, before giving peace to your surroundings, you must he in peace yourself. First, face your lack of peace. See that you are constantly at war with yourself, you are violent and aggressive with yourself. As long as there is an ego, there is war. As long as you think you're an independent entity, there's war, and it's useless to try to end conflict on a social level. If you are not in harmony with yourself, you remain an accomplice to society.

This question of war and peace is very important. When you come to the life experience of global being, there is real freedom and absolute security. As long as you have not integrated this freedom you cannot help bring social or political freedom. Freedom can never come through a system.

Q. But we need to influence institutions. How can we do that?
A. Don't try to influence. The moment you breathe, the whole world is affected by your inhalation and exhalation. So when you live in peace you radiate it. If someone

asks for help, help of course. But don't become a professional do-gooder.

Q. Doesn't one have a personal responsibility to change things one feels are wrong?
A. When you are free from the idea of being somebody, the problem of responsibility doesn't play a role. When you are no longer limited by the personality, there is intelligence, and acting is adequate from moment to moment.

If you have any idea of being somebody, a friend, helper, political person, teacher, mother, father, and so on, you will only see the situation coloured by this image. It is a fractional view and because it is partial it breeds conflict and reaction. Since the action did not appear and disappear in wholeness there will be residue. Before acting, one must understand the situation. To fully comprehend it, you must face the facts free from ideas. It must belong to your wholeness; otherwise you are stuck to the wheel of reaction where there is only relationship from concept to concept.

When you become a professional doer you are no longer spontaneous. You can never create harmony. It is beautiful to be really nothing, without qualification. All that appears, appears in you and you act according to the appearance using your capital, intellectual, bodily, material, etc. Then all action is balanced.

Q. You say don't become a professional do-gooder but what if that is my job? Also, I know that you yourself travel the globe doing good. We cannot just sit and let people suffer! No one who is starving is interested in self-inquiry. Biological survival must be taken care of first. This requires professionals.
A. I don't say you must ignore the world but first you have

to know how to face the facts properly, that is, free from the limited individual point of view. Our surroundings appear to us according to the stance we take. From the point of view of the body and senses, the world appears as sense perception. From the mental view the world appears as mind. From consciousness the world is only consciousness. When you leave here don't try to change anything. Only be aware that your ideas and actions stem from the mind. The moment you look at your surroundings from consciousness you will see things differently and seeing things differently your understanding and actions will be different. You can never change the world from the personal standpoint. You can only change society from the impersonal, from consciousness. The question often arises: how can I change society, I disagree with so many things? Realise that there can be no transformation unless action comes from a completely different view than before. In the personal realm you remain an accomplice with society. Creative action can only come when you see your surroundings from the point of view of consciousness. Then you are really related to society, the situation, the world. Otherwise, you remain related only to yourself, your reactions and resistances. See that society begins with you.

You are your own nearest environment, so begin with yourself. When you learn how to look at your closest environment you will automatically know how to look at the broader environment. In this way of looking there's understanding, and understanding brings right acting. The moment you come to the living understanding, you won't need to ask me or anyone else what to do.

Q. Isn't there work to be done to improve communication and dialogue between different countries?

A. What is communication? As so-called communication has grown, has war decreased? First learn to communicate with yourself and your nearest surroundings. Clean your own room and make it ready for the guests. When there is order and harmony in one society it affects the whole world. Becoming a professional do-gooder is an escape from facing one's own field. It is only a camouflage. But of course if the opportunity to help comes, never refuse.

Q. But surely we need goals in life?
A. Where there's an ego there is purpose. And when there is no sense of 'I', there is no purpose. Life is purposeless. There's only beauty in living in the eternal. If you believe you are the individual 'I' you are isolated from your surroundings, and this isolation brings feelings of insecurity, fear and anxiety. Then you look for goals. You worry and anticipate. Life doesn't need a reason to be. That is its beauty.

Q. How can I deal with the sufferings of others?
A. When seen deeply, there is no difference between your suffering and the suffering of the environment because both are equally objects of perception. It is through your body that you come near to the suffering of the environment. All suffering points to the ultimate perceiver. See it this way, not through justification and blaming. All justification is an escape from reality, a refusal. It is only when you really make suffering an object of perception and do not project it as belonging to others that you liberate yourself and others from it.

Q. Is there any accident in life?
A. There's no accident because everything that happens belongs to the whole. From the personal point of view it

may appear accidental or coincidental, but in the divine eye of infinity there's only simultaneity.

Q. In wholeness we cannot talk about fate or determinism, can we?

A. There is no past, present or future. The future is a projected past and the present is past the moment you think of it. All happens in your presence, which is timeless. Fatalism is a passive attitude where you are given over to the situation, identified with it. But you are not the situation, the film, but the light which illuminates and gives life to it. What you call an accident, fate, etc., is in the film but you, the light, are not.

Q. What do you mean 'in the film'? Is this not determinism in some way?

A. Determinism is linear but there is no one creation of world history. The world is created every moment out of all possibilities. All possibilities are in you – why identify with one expression? All relativity only has meaning in your wholeness.

When there is only simultaneity then everything happens at every moment. Past, present and future come together in presence. Only from consciousness, globality, can the film be seen in its entirety. Otherwise you remain bound to fractions, to the different images, and you go into each picture. The content of your life is more than you know. When there is clarity and discernment your attention and energy will no longer be lived and dispersed in images.

Q. What is the foundation for a truly religious life?

A. It is not in changing your life-style or adopting a new formula or philosophy but in discovering the ultimate limits of thinking and becoming. When the mind is exhausted it comes to its inherent calmness. In this tranquillity reality is reflected and is experienced as a fore-feeling. The fore-feeling must unfold to living reality, to what has been fore-felt. One could call it an involution to the source of the fore-feeling. However, the realising of the fore-feeling cannot be an idea based on hearsay; rather, you must be taken by reality, absorbed totally by it in direct experience. This is not only the foundation for a religious life, but the foundation for a whole new society, a humanity in beauty and love.

KNOWING YOURSELF

To be free from the idea of being someone –
that is illumination

The human form is a microcosm of the universe. All that supposedly exists outside us in reality exists in us. The world is in you and can become known in you, as you. What then is this 'you'?

As a human being related to all living beings we must first be related to ourselves. We cannot understand, love and welcome others without first knowing and loving ourselves. Generally, however, we spend our whole lives involved in what is apparently outside us without ever looking at what is closest. We give no time to the thorough reading of our own book, our reactions, resistances, tensions, emotional states, physical stresses and so on. This reading requires no system or specially allotted time spent in introspection. It involves only facing oneself during the day without the habitual identification with an individual centre of reference, an I-image, a personality, a propagator of viewpoints.

To face ourselves scientifically we must accept the facts as they are without agreement, disagreement or conclusion. It is not a mental acceptance, an acceptance of ideas, but is completely practical, functional. It requires only alertness. Attention must be bipolar. We see the situation and at the same time see how it echoes in us as feeling and thought. In other words, the facts of a situation must include our own reactions. We remain in the scientific process free from judgement, interpretation and evaluation, only looking in different moments of the day, at our psychological, intellectual and physical ground and our level of vitality. There is no motive, no interference from a 'me', no desire to change, grow or become. Functional acceptance is not moral. There is no need to opt for a new way of living which, inevitably, becomes a system like any other. When attention is bipolar, at first there is observation of the so-called outer world but with an emphasis on inner movements. Then these movements, the likes and dislikes, themselves become the object of exploration. In this way we become more intimate with ourselves, more aware of how we function from moment to moment in everyday life. When we are explorers, real listening appears automatically and in listening there is openness, receptivity. Exploration never becomes a fixation with a goal to be achieved. It remains as a welcoming that brings originality and life to every moment.

Many therapies tell us to accept ourselves but this psychological acceptance, through various kinds of analysis, always refers to an individual centre. As long as the idea of the individual remains, there is a hidden motive in the accepting. It is not unconditional acceptance but is based on an ideal, or comparison, and always contains an element of resignation. Psychology believes in the existence of the ego and its task is to make the ego more comfortable, stronger or integrated. That we can arrange life more satisfyingly is something, but it can never be a way to take us beyond the known. Such processes keep us interested in the object no matter how subtle it becomes. In functional acceptance the emphasis is not on what we accept but on acceptance itself.

There is nothing to try to add or subtract from the life you are living. It takes only alertness to see habits of thinking and how these contract us. When we see that almost all of our existence is mechanical repetition we automatically step out of the pattern and into observing. All attempts to alter ourselves are based on interpretation which assumes the existence of an interpreter, but when there is no one to interpret, no individual centre of reference, the emphasis falls spontaneously on taking note itself. It is important to realise that this observing without an agent is not an attitude or a state. The object is not interesting. Observing itself has its own taste and needs no addition. It is the same openness, welcoming, that is our natural being.

To come into true relation with oneself and thus the world, all psychological interferences must cease. It is the observer who, constantly projecting acquired knowledge and desires, maintains the observed as object and thus destroys all true communication, which is love. With the disappearance of the habit of being someone doing something, only naked attention remains and in its light the functioning of projection is made clear. The mind regains its natural sensitivity and flexibility and at the same time we feel freedom in relation to our environment. In open exploration, where you accept yourself scientifically, the day will come when you feel yourself completely autonomous and fulfilled without qualification.

Q. I'm not sure what you mean exactly by distinguishing 'psychological' from 'functional' acceptance.
A. In psychological acceptance there is still somebody who accepts. There is a point of view, a choice, or a motive and goal. So there is still complicity, an invested interest in what you supposedly accept. This interest binds you to the object, the anger, anxiety, jealousy, the demon, hero, goddess, and so on, and you remain functionally

passive in regard to it. You submit to it. You say 'I am this' and try to welcome it. Psychological acceptance is a subtle kind of sacrifice.

Functional acceptance is a completely non-affective position because it is from the beginning ego-free, that is, free from all mental interference. It is primarily active. By this, I mean there is complete alertness in taking note. There is no submission to the object. There is only welcoming it without analysis of any kind. In other words – you step directly out of the becoming process into openness itself.

Q. Is this openness the subject aspect?
A. Pedagogically speaking there is a shift away from emphasising the object towards the so-called subject, the perceiving itself. However, the great danger is to emphasise the subject, to make it an object, substantial in some way, and then you have assumed an attitude and you are back in becoming. Real acceptance is openness free from all objectification.

Q. It is like the man in prison who files away at his bars year after year and as each one disappears so his hopes and dreams of freedom grow. The actual fact is that as long as there is one bar he is just as much a prisoner as he was with all of them, and freedom is still an idea.
A. Openness is alertness without any expectation. Observation must simply remain with the facts.

Q. If I give no attention to the aspects of the ego, may there not be the danger of repressing them?
A. Observation is not directed to the object, the object appears in observation. When you allow the aspects of the body-mind to appear in your multidimensional attention they come up like mist out of the valley and are burned

up in the heat of the sun. Nothing is left to be repressed and there is no one to repress. It is a completely new way of living. When you live in openness all appears and disappears in it.

Q. You said that it is not the object of exploration that is attractive but the nature of exploring itself. Sometimes I have moments of sadness because I have been exploring for twenty years without coming to the absolute conviction that there is nothing to explore.

A. You must explore as long as you need to explore. But once you start emphasising the object of exploration, the anecdotal, you may never come to the end of it. The world is infinite variety and there is the danger that you become more and more taken by the object. *Maya* can be very subtle and deceptive and lure you into wonderful states and intuitions but you remain in the world of duality, never coming to see the real nature of existence. So if you explore what you are not without the immediate background of what you are, you are stepping onto a road that may take more years than you have in a lifetime. But when the emphasis is on the openness itself, the object becomes transparent and its transparency refers directly to your non-objective openness. Very quickly you understand that this is the real nature of the object, of all existence, and you find yourself in this welcoming and no longer in a supposedly concrete object.

You do not need to know the details of the ego, only its nature. If you bite into rotten fruit you know it is bad, you don't need to eat it all to make sure! Nothing new can be learned by pursuing the known. The Desert Fathers used to say, 'Know yourself and forget yourself.'

Q. How can I welcome directly from wholeness without first knowing what it is?

A. The moment the mind does not interfere you are ego-free. There's no need to think of the ego. In welcoming you are already in wholeness. Accept it second-hand and proceed to prove it yourself.

Q. Accepting it second-hand amounts to having faith, doesn't it?

A. Yes, but you must discover what faith is. It is not belief. In accepting that you are consciousness you are open to a new dimension. It is important to place faith in truth. When what you accept is vital you will be brought to the living proof. Faith must be informed, not blind. Faith is not beyond your possibilities of knowing. It is knowing how to face facts by surrendering desire and will. It has nothing to do with dependency but brings you to greater and greater autonomy.

Q. If the ego is not real – that is, autonomous and continuous, what is it that functions in everyday life?

A. The ego has no concreteness, no substance, no continuity. It is a collection of thoughts held together by memory. The person appears when you think of it. When the body wakes up in the morning, awareness is already there. You may not have noticed it but it is so. This awareness is not a thought, not a subject, nor a feeling. It finds no concretisation. Moments later, habit associates awareness with a body and a personality. Then you say, 'I am this. I am that.'

We may call this awareness without object, consciousness, the ultimate subject or the unconditional 'I'. This unconditional 'I' is the alertness that welcomes all the parasites of this and that. The thought of being a certain person limits the inbuilt intelligence of mind and body.

When you are simply alert and dissociated from your habits of believing in a personality, then all your capacities can come into play when stimulated by a situation. There is only action, no actor who acts. You function far more imaginatively, broadly and efficiently with all your intelligence and talents.

Q. Where does the ego originate?
A. The ego, consciousness of oneself as an individual, is only one concept among many. It is created by society, parents and education and crystallises as a complex of data and experiences. There is no one ego that can be described. Rather, there are two, three, a thousand 'me's'. You may have a different set of characteristics to your neighbour but this collection of characteristics is not you. Each 'me' corresponds to a different situation but since memory retains the 'me' long after the situation is over, the various egos are often in conflict in the collection we call the personality. There is no possibility of circumscribing the aggregate of memorised 'me's' and when you see that it is an object, perceivable like others, you will find that it is not a constant. The idea of an ego which occupies a psychic centre is an assumption. Take away all the characteristics, all that you believe yourself to be, all that is phenomenal, and what is left? No-thing, simply being, stillness, presence. Why then spend a lifetime exploring the realm of the illusory ego and its projections? Why not go directly to what you are?

Q. You sometimes use the words *unconscious, subconscious* and *archetype*. What do these mean for you?
A. Unconscious and subconscious still belong to existence. We cannot separate fractions of existence from the whole of existence. All that exists belongs to existence. Archetypes are non-articulated existence, like the depths

of the ocean. They are the root source – as pools, rivers, streams, the oceans all belong to the element we call water. It may help to see the roots of existence but your real life is the ground in which the roots are growing.

When the object unfolds in you and you are no longer living in the city of memory, you are open to cosmic memory, the all-possible, and collective memory may come up. The archetypes, root symbols, remain and you become more sensitive to them. You feel them as original power, condensed life expression. When the water is clear, the unmoving objects on the bottom show through.

Q. What are dreams?
A. Sometimes what we postpone during the day emerges in a dream. It is an elimination and appears more or less successively like perceptions in the waking state. But there are spontaneous appearances called *songes* in French which do not go through the ordinary brain function. They appear simultaneously in the interval between deep sleep and waking. You might see your whole life in a flash. There may be elements which belong to the composition of the whole which later, in the waking state, you call the future.

Q. Can we interpret dreams?
A. It is very dangerous to interpret these dreams through the waking state. More interesting is to observe how you feel on waking and live with the echo of the dream without objectifying the elements in it. In *songes* the cosmos dreams in you. The dreaming and waking states are more or less the same. While you are dreaming the story is real for you. Only later do you call it a dream. What makes you so certain you are not dreaming now?

Q. Even when one is no longer identified with the personality there's still functioning, so in some sense the personality must be there.

A. When you are free from the self-image there is only alertness, stillness free from agitation. There is only listening from moment to moment. So where is there room for an image, a subject and an object, someone who knows something? In this openness, function takes place in your awareness but there is no 'you' in the function.

Q. But aren't there still preferences of that functioning body?

A. The body takes itself in charge. It doesn't need a controller. What you call the personality is an inflexible accumulation of emotive images. The real personality appears in your stillness only when you need it and disappears when the situation no longer calls for it. It is flexible without a periphery. It is multidimensional, free from psychological interference. When you are called upon to be a mother, a father, a lover, a student, a teacher, a fighter, you are these temporarily, but they do not remain as a state you identify with. Then there is love, there is affection without affectivity.

It is very interesting and beautiful to live with your surroundings in a way where there is no repetition. The man, woman or child you live with is always new because you are always new. There is no projection of an image onto your companion and he or she feels free in your freedom.

Q. Earlier you mentioned the capacities that come into play when the ego, the person, is absent. Are these capacities inherited or learned and, if not, where do they come from?

A. The real personality is not personal. This transpersonality, if we can call it that, utilises an intelligence and sensitivity that are universal. Genetics and learning are a very small part of our full capacities. Adequate acting belongs to the situation of the moment. The transpersonality is open to every possibility.

Q. Why is the drive to associate unconditioned awareness with an ego so strong?
A. The idea of an ego is millions of years old. It comes from the desire to distinguish yourself from other beings, to feel yourself as an independent entity. Once you take yourself for a separate individual, you can only find yourself in connection with things, with the perceived. The ego needs situations for its survival, and when there are no happenings, it feels its insecurity and strives to create more. This is why you cannot live the moments of stillness between thoughts and activities. You live in psychological survival. So, come to know yourself as you are before your body wakes up. Come to know yourself as you are before you are born.

Q. How then can I become free from this limitation, the sense of being an individual entity?
A. First welcome all that you think you are. When you fully welcome all that you take as yourself, you will suddenly find yourself in openness and you will see that this, and not your assumptions about your character and so on, is your real nature. In openness you are aware that all you think, all that appears, is not you. When you welcome the body, senses and mind, and find that they are only objects of your perception which appear in you, you discover a new dimension behind your beliefs. You will be absorbed by this new dimension and will see that what you took to be yourself is only an expression of what you are. Then you live completely integrated,

knowingly in your totality.

This coming to know what you are not is an organic ripening but it can happen in one moment. There is great beauty in it.

Q. What do you mean by 'organic ripening but it can happen in one moment'?
A. The ripening is not time-bound in the sense of becoming. It can happen in the time it takes to have one thought. When you know all you are not, what you are appears instantaneously and is not a thought.

Q. What is the importance of organic ripeness?
A. It happens sometimes that your natural being appears but you make a state of it, you objectify it. In this appearing you are one and your body, senses and mind are struck in every corner. However, when you are ripe, have intellectual understanding and are thus open to the unknown, open to being astonished, then wonder vanishes in causeless being. Otherwise you may be taken by the newness and remain bound to the object.

Life is a laboratory. Live more and more intimately with yourself. Listening is love. When you sustain welcoming it attracts you to itself and the emphasis is no longer on the sensation but on welcoming.

Q. How can I sustain the welcoming without somehow concentrating on it to some degree?
A. Sustaining without concentration happens spontaneously when there is no agent, no sustainer. In the absence of a director who is interested in the object, the emphasis falls on the looking, welcoming, itself, and the object is set free. In other words, at the moment of taking note there is *only* taking note and nothing to note. The object is really only fixed energy and the release of the energy

happens suddenly, unexpectedly. In this relinquishment, all energy is reorchestrated and brought back to its original state of movement without direction.

Q. You said the freeing of the object comes unexpectedly. Would you say more about this?
A. There are different layers in what we normally call a feeling or sensation. As looking without conclusion is sustained, the sensation unfolds and the deeper layers, freed from tension, come up.

This unfolding cannot be produced. It is welcoming that is the magnet. The full unfolding of the object takes place when you listen more and more to the welcoming and less to the sensation, the object. In the end you feel a sudden transference where the residues of emphasis on the object vanish in looking, alertness, openness. It is a kind of implosion where the so-called object is absorbed in awareness.

Q. What is the origin of this ignorance of our real nature?
A. It's simply a forgetting. When a child is in a market at Christmas he is completely absorbed in the toys and forgets his mother, but there comes a moment when he remembers her. The objective world is very attractive and as long as you are not interested in reality, it hides behind name and form. When you take away form and name what remains? The *Upanishads* say the divine is shy like a gazelle, and of course the Tao that can be named is not the Tao.

Q. Why is it so difficult to realise our inner being?
A. There is nothing to be realised. When you think of realising, you project non-realising. When you say difficult, you project its opposite, easy. There is no destination,

no interiorisation. Because you see thoughts, feelings and sensations as inside you, you identify with them. You must come to see that the body is an object of observation exactly as a tree is. Then there is no inside and outside and no preference for identification. In the natural state there is no inner and outer. All these are concepts. Simply be open to all perception. Things appear in this openness, point to openness and vanish in openness. There is no grasping and identification. There is only happening. All that appears points to your real nature.

Thought, language, is dualistic, it is true, but you must learn to use it correctly and it will bring clarity.

Q. Why do we continually identify with concepts?
A. Take away the why. The why is an escape. See the pattern. The why doesn't bring any solution. Questions like, 'Why does the world exist? Why do I exist?' can never be answered. When the why comes to an end, you are out of the circle of memory.

In living with your question, you are without expectation. This living is multidimensional. It is simply listening without any goal. In this motiveless observation, the question unfolds and you are in a new dimension.

Q. Why do I resist freedom?
A. Who resists? Look at the mechanism. As long as you live in like and dislike, the pain-pleasure structure, you'll find resistance. Ultimate satisfaction comes when the perceiver loses all volition. When attention loses its grasping, volitional quality, the perceived is freed and dissolved in the perceiver. But the perceiver must first be free of all will in order for the perceived to be released. In the Kashmir tradition the perceiver is Shiva and the perceived is Parvati, or Shakta and Shakti. When Shakta still retains residues of will and Shakti is not completely

freed, you have the moment which may be compared with St. John of the Cross's 'Dark Night of the Soul', where the object no longer interests you but is still not completely unfolded. Energy is not freely flowing. It is a terrible period where volition has lost its dynamism, the world has lost its charm, but energy is not fully integrated. It is important to see that resistance is only an idea. The image of being somebody is very deeply rooted. It is the image which refuses.

Q. What is it that moves us to search?
A. The longing to find yourself. Your true nature attracts you even without your knowing it.

Q. Where does the ardour come from to proceed in self-inquiry?
A. When you see your mechanism, released energy springs up which brings you to see things still more clearly and to live this clarity. There will come a time when you feel that all the directions you have taken to look for freedom, peace and happiness have disappointed you. Then the dynamism to strive comes to a standstill and there is a fore-feeling of your real nature. The fore-feeling comes directly from what is forefelt.

With the fore-feeling, you will be spontaneously orientated. All energy previously expended in searching outside on different paths will be reorchestrated. Of course this takes a certain maturity. But inquiry with deepest interest brings you to this maturity. It appears when you question life and live with the question without interpretation or conclusion. At a certain point the question dissolves into the answer from which it comes. In the question is the fore-feeling of the answer.

Q. I find in my life that I'm lazy in self-inquiry and though there's a certain calling, I don't really follow it through earnestly. What can I do?

A. In your way of looking there is repetition. Where there's repetition there is boredom and laziness. You must explore. Exploring means that the already known must come to a stop. You must be as new to life as a child. You must become acquainted with listening to yourself and your surroundings. Take a deep interest in your own story. Face your reactions. Every time you face your reaction you cease to be an accomplice with it and without fuel it fades away. Generally when you say, 'I know this person, poem, painting,' what you know is only a reaction of some kind to it. But when you live free from all reaction you find yourself in a new dimension that is always interesting! In life you must make a choice and the choice should be to live in beauty. So become more acquainted with beauty.

Q. I find it hard to escape intention, the intention to relax, to be clear, peaceful, and so on. Would you talk more about non-intentional observation?

A. Real observation is completely unfurnished of ideals and ideas. To be free from intention is to be free of direction. It is being multidimensional. It has nothing to do with concentration which looks for a result. In real observation you function like the scientist who takes note without psychological interference. The scientist as a person, an attitude, is completely absent and in this emptiness pure attention is a magnet to which observations *a, b* and *c* are, at a certain point, attracted like metal pieces. In the same way, if you take note without analysis and criticism, there will be a sudden becoming aware. At first you will feel it during a reaction, then before the reaction and later at the moment of the impulse to react.

Then there will come a time when you are free even of the impulse to react.

Be careful that observation remains purely functional. There is often the reflex to create an attitude of detachment. This psychological gap has nothing to do with being the witness. Very often when we think we see a situation clearly, we have merely invented a psychological objectivity. This distancing is the work of the self-image and is still reaction. Reactionless observation can never be a thought, an attitude you learn. It has nothing to do with the analytical process. It goes through a completely new channel and the conclusion is instantaneous.

Q. How can we discriminate between observation that is still mental and the thought-free observation you are talking about?
A. You might want to say, 'I know I am not the body, senses and mind,' but before you can really say this, you must see clearly what it is that you are not. As you listen more and more to your body-mind there comes a sensation of distancing that has nothing to do with psychological detachment. In this spaciousness, the fore-feeling of your autonomy, of your being aware, comes up. When you make your psychosomatic structure an object of observation there is at first a space relation between observing and observed. However, there comes a time when the object of observation, your psychosomatic structure, is no longer emphasised, and you find the emphasis on listening itself. Then there is the understanding that you are not the body, but the body, the object, lives in you, in your awareness. This is what is meant by saying the observed is in the observer but the observer is not in the observed, creation is in God but God is not in creation. When you look at an object, turn your head and see the source of looking. Be aware that you are the light of all perception.

Q. Is this source that you turn to see, the ultimate subject, your real nature?
A. Be very careful. The subject that can be seen is not your homeground. What is sometimes called the ultimate subject is nothing other than silence, *sunyata*, emptiness of images. This is consciousness, the light behind all perception. The subject that is talked about is still in duality, the subject-object relationship.

Q. Is this freedom permanent?
A. Yes. It is continuity. It remains in everyday actions. You do your work and you are presence. This continuity is not an object of observation since consciousness is not divided. Nor is it a state. It is the timeless source from which the waking, dreaming and sleeping states emanate and into which they are reabsorbed. It is the background to the thinking state. It has never changed, nor does it ever change.

Q. Was it before I was born?
A. Who told you you were born? Your mother? It is second-hand information. Do *you* know you are born? No! You can say that a sensation, a perception is born and dies but you can never say that you are born.

Q. Then I cannot ask you if the state of pure being continues after death?
A. A state is an experience. What you are is not an experience. Freedom is causeless, not a condition. It doesn't belong to existence. Existence is in space and time.

Q. But how shall I view death?
A. Why speak of death when you don't know life? Don't live with second-hand information. When you know what life is, the question of death is irrelevant. Life is causeless

– it can never be born. So why speak of death? You die at every moment. You die every evening when you go to sleep. When you go from the dreaming to the waking state you die. Everything dies immediately. When you know this dying you will know that life, consciousness, always is.

Q. How does one become spontaneous?
A. To discover spontaneity one must go beyond the conventional morality fixed by society. Spontaneity is love and springs from the highest intelligence and integration. It is living moment by moment in the supreme art of self-surrender where conflict is unknown. Action which proceeds from thought, habit, emotion, blind urges and instinct is compulsive and cannot possibly be spontaneous. Spontaneity springs from meditative stillness. It cannot he pursued; no system or technique can teach you spontaneity. In fact one quickly becomes dependent on methods of exclusion and discipline and they lead to a state of reduced sensitivity and automatic and mechanical behaviour. In watchfulness and listening the mind undergoes a penetrating transformation where the intellect sees its limits and is illumined, no longer confused, restless and self-centred. It becomes silent, meditating. Conscious and unconscious agitation must come to an end through observation and understanding for spontaneity to take place. If we go to the source of our actions in the past, we find out how the hidden urges of the subconscious mind deny the spontaneous action that springs from freedom. Then there is a transmutation of our basic nature, its deepest urges and instincts, and energy becomes integrated in completeness, in being.

The ending of the becoming process is the beginning of spontaneity. Spontaneity is fullness of energy. It is love.

Q. Is not the traditional Japanese art of archery or flower arranging or calligraphy a technique that teaches spontaneity?

A. Strictly speaking it is not a technique. A technique is when you adopt something, a system to come nearer to a goal. But spontaneous painting or archery depend only on looking away from the goal, on action free from all volition.

Q. What is boredom and how can I become free from it?

A. If we live superficially and take note that we do, we may become aware of a deep lack or discomfort, a disease, which we call boredom. Rather than face these moments of boredom, we go from one compensation to another to fill in the lack. But if we really face these moments, really perceive them without justifying, conceptualising or analysing them, a transformation takes place. The boredom must be allowed to remain as pure perception, as feeling, sensation. The perception is real and if it is allowed to unfold, it will blossom in stillness and point to awareness.

Too often we interfere with the perception and qualify it, at once making it a concept. A concept is not real but a product of the mind and as such it can teach nothing nor point to anything other than old mental patterns and memory. If you free the perception from the hold of the ego, you will find that the energy that was blocked, localised into fixed patterns, becomes freed and is reorchestrated. Every circumstance is new when the mind does not impose the old onto it. So each situation calls for a reharmonising of energy which is perfectly appropriate to the situation. In this reharmonising, all the energy that was previously dispersed in memory, habits, psychological time, dissolves in our timeless presence.

Q. Is there a correct and incorrect way to act?
A. Right action does not come from the personality. It springs from the situation itself and as such leaves no residue. Just as the answer is in the question, so the solution to a situation lies in the situation. When the personality does not dictate action, or, strictly speaking, reaction, you will find yourself completely adequate to the situation. Correct action is simply function. Very often the intuition of right action is not pleasant for the self-image which, feeling threatened, doubts or quarrels with the spontaneous intuition. It takes courage for the abdication of the person to happen.

Q. What do you mean by 'leaves no residue'?
A. Reaction is non-accomplished action. The residue of this non-accomplishment remains in you as memory. Where there is no actor there can be no residue. Action that springs from global awareness of a situation is automatically right action. It is free from intention and motive. Right or correct action does not refer to a psychological state, a morality, but to function inspired directly by the situation. Such action is always spontaneous, is not related to memory and leaves no residue. It cannot be repeated. Reaction is conditioned by memory and is always impulsive or compulsive.

Q. Can right action leave residue in others?
A. It is possible that the action may be misinterpreted by those who do not see the whole situation, who look from a point of view.

But you can be sure that sooner or later it will be clearly seen as coming from a global background. Simple function is harmonious because it springs from harmony. It arises from love. Right action is worthy from moment to moment, not just in its completion.

Q. Is it possible to have right action limited by human error?

A. Intelligent action belongs to your resources. It does not go beyond them. Right motive looks for right action. Of course you may need the tools to execute the action. Asking others to help is part of the action. Right action calls for continual reassessment of your capital, intellectual, physical, etc. Where there is functional error even if the ground of love is there, it cannot strictly speaking be called right action.

Q. What do you call the urge of the Bodhisattva to teach and enlighten all beings if there is no intention in right doing?

A. Intention comes from the idea of being a separate individual. When the ego is dissolved and one's infinite nature is realised there is great thankfulness. Thankfulness is thanking love for love. It overflows in offering, in compassion and love for others. But sympathy and pity are accomplices with suffering.

Q. From where comes the feeling of responsibility?

A. When you offer what you deeply are to others, responsibility does not enter the picture. Your doing is free from duty, obligation, morality. All your action is spontaneously responsible. It comes out of thankfulness and love but there is no one who acts, no feeling of responsibility.

Q. Where does desire come from?

A. All desire is ultimately the search for peace and as such springs from desirelessness. When a desired thing is attained there is a moment of desirelessness without subject and object. Later, we attribute this contentment to the object but in the moment itself there is no cause and effect, no perceiver and perceived. We are on our home-ground. All desire springs from the urge to be at home permanently.

What is generally called desire is a psychological superimposition created by the ego for its survival. Most desire comes from psychological memory, that fortress of the ego. Of course, there is desire which comes from the body itself. It belongs to biological survival and is a natural function.

Q. Would you speak about stimulation?
A. Your completeness is autonomous. That means there is no need for stimulation to fill a lack. A certain amount of stimulation is important for the biological structure, of course, otherwise it dies. But because this appears within your real nature you are not bound by its appearing. It holds no interest for you in itself. All appears in consciousness. Biological stimulation is then jubilation; existence is only play. It is an expression of wholeness. When you are consciousness you see, feel, taste, hear only consciousness. All need springs from lack and almost all our need for stimulation stems from mental confusion.

Q. I often find myself trying to repeat certain experiences or sensations which were pleasurable. Why is this?
A. The person needs experiences to exist and looks to repeat them. Pleasure offers more security for the ego than pain. As long as you take yourself for an experiencer you live in the pleasure-pain cycle. Objectless consciousness, your real nature, is joy without experiencer or experience. It is not connected to time, memory, feeling or sensation, so there is nothing to repeat. You are the guest of joy, you cannot impose yourself.

Q. Would you clarify the distinction between joy and pleasure?

A. Pleasure is always in the shadow of pain. In joy there is no counterpart. Joy is without cause or object. As all appears in joy, pleasure too appears in joy. Joy is the background out of which the opposites, pleasure and pain, arise, and into which they reduce. Pleasure maintains the person whilst joy annihilates the person. Joy may appear spontaneously but often it degenerates into pleasure.

Q. How does this degeneration occur?
A. You conceptualise joy. Joy is global, but what is conceptualised becomes successive since there cannot be more than one concept at a time. Pleasure is fractional. Joy is multidimensional. Pleasure has a beginning and an end but joy is continuous.

Q. Would you say joy is the synthesis of pleasure and pain?
A. Joy is all-encompassing. It is the source, not the synthesis, of fractions. The 'still joy' I speak of is a living principle. Existence, pleasure and pain are in this joy but it is not bound to them. Where there is a conceptual – and not a living – principle there is no warmth, no life.

Q. I have such a hectic life it is difficult to try to relax.
A. Don't try to relax. When you try, you automatically project old patterns, because the striver is part of that which he tries to overcome. To come to deeper layers of peace we must listen to the body. When you come to innocent, unconditional listening, your body goes spontaneously into deep peace. The body has an organic memory of peace when you let it function. But you constantly interfere with it in one way or another, by thoughts, desires, emotions and goals.

Come to know your capital, your resources. Live

within your means. Eat when the body asks you for food. Rest when it asks for rest.

Q. But I am having some tremendous difficulties in my life and find that I cannot accept them as you say. How can I handle this conflict?

A. From the moment you explore the proper meaning of the word 'surrender' you will taste real freedom because surrender frees you from the object, the feeling of depression and conflict, and at the same time it points to the openness itself. That is the essence of surrender and is your real nature. Surrender calls for a true recognition of the facts, facing them squarely. You must accept and welcome them in a scientific way without reaction and judgement. Accepting is not a sacrifice nor a process of will. In the openness that is inherent in our nature there is no one who accepts. Acceptance or surrender is thus passive in its absence of a director and active in that one remains supremely awake and alert, ready for what presents itself. This silence is simply waiting without the anxiety of waiting and in this openness the highest intelligence operates.

Be aware, take note of the reflex to fight, suppress, change, reform or sublimate a problem. That will only lead you deeper into conflict. In non-acceptance you stay involved in the object, bound to it. The appropriate solution to a problem can only appear in the absence of the ego, the perpetrator of likes and dislikes. The ego often shuns the solution that presents itself, saying, 'I don't like it. It does not give me pleasure.' It is important to watch that when a solution appears, the ego does not steal it and hide it.

In taking the emphasis off the problem and putting it on acceptance you will find that the pressure dissolves and calm and relaxation comes to you. Every problem has its solution even though the mind and its memory cannot fully comprehend the problem or the solution. In surrendering to the problem you are open to the known and the unknown in the problematic situation and understanding operates freshly. In silent surrender there is bliss and prayer without request or demand. There is no doer, experiencer, lover or beloved. There is only a divine current. You see that the very act of welcoming is itself the solution to the problem and the action which follows your comprehension is very straightforward. When you become familiar with the act of surrender, truth will solicit you unsought.

Q. I feel so many negative parts to myself. How can I welcome what is ugly?
A. Don't compare yourself with your neighbour. You are a unique link in the totality of humanity. When you compare, you judge and feel guilty. Look at your mechanism directly without reference to an image. When there is no projection of a result, you face your naked psychosomatic field. You'll be surprised that when you face your naked field without judgement, there is nothing negative in it.

Q. But I don't always compare myself with my neighbour. I have an inner feeling of what harmony and beauty is and I feel I fall short of it.
A. All negative feelings are comparison based on memory. Moments of harmony and beauty come from your home-ground, what you are, and strike your whole being. The ego is struck and, feeling its imminent death, steals the moment for itself. The ego is a thief which appropriates all to itself. Moments of peace leave a lasting perfume in you but the mind conceptualises this and makes it an ideal. You are then living in the foolish position of comparing yourself with a caricature of what you really are.

Q. So it is only in functional acceptance that I can face my psychosomatic ground without comparison?

A. Yes, face it in action, not with the mind. Then there can be no comparison. Comparison is a mental activity. Only in facing it is transformation possible. In the *Bhagavadgita* Arjuna was tempted away from the field of action for reasons which were unpleasant for him personally, but Krishna showed him that all his reasons were based on memory. In welcoming, there is no centre, no self-image, and the vision of the whole can come to you. Action is then free and appropriate. In welcoming, the old patterns will come up but when you don't fall into them there comes a moment of release. This release is the unfolding of the pattern, the freeing of fixed energy which then blossoms in and enlivens your accepting position.

Q. Is there any value in trying to think positively?

A. Positive thinking belongs to psychological survival. It is the affirmation of the ego. Psychological technique reinforces experience and experiencer. But as long as you still live in the mind, in complementarity, then positive thinking is closer to your real nature than negative thinking. However, all such methods are crutches to help you walk in apparent security. They are supports for the immature. When you live in wholeness, you have no need for such supports. It is like the tight-rope walker who has found perfect balance without aid. If someone comes to the right or left and offers help he is no longer at ease because his balance does not refer to left or right.

Q. I'm afraid of the nothingness I'll be faced with if the personality dies.

A. You are accustomed to living in fraction. When the self-image dies you live in completeness. This fullness can never be objectified because there's no agent left to think it. It can only be lived. You must familiarise yourself with dying. It's a new feeling. A feeling without feeling.

You imagine that the death of the I-image is an absence. But this is only the ego speaking on behalf of its own survival. Come out of the vicious circle of living in the narrow world of the ego. True death of the insecure ego leaves you in complete security. So what is insecurity from the point of view of the relative 'I' is absolute security in terms of your whole being. There are people living in tragic situations but they prefer to live this way rather than in no situation at all because where there is no situation there is no more hold for the 'me'.

Q. Is all fear then based on a fractional view?
A. Yes. Because a fraction is isolated. It is separation from totality. This separation brings up fear and anxiety. Fear and who is afraid are one, not two.

Q. But how can I face fear in the moment when it comes up?
A. Be aware that fear is not fearsome. The word 'fear' is powerful. As soon as you pronounce it, it stimulates a neurochemical change. So give up the concept of fear and you'll be left facing the perception, the sensation. When you name something you go away from it in its nakedness and endow it with all the accoutrements of memory.

Practically speaking, when you face the sensation you will find it localised somewhere in your body. You will feel it as tension, contraction. As soon as you locate the tension, go away from it; otherwise there's the danger of fixating on it. Go away, not in escape which is mental, but to the areas around that are free and relaxed. Go into the healthy surrounding parts and let their lightness infiltrate the tense areas. What you name fear is only fixed energy. You must free the energy.

Q. Is there not a sensation we call fear which comes from biological survival?
A. When you are in danger, the body takes itself in charge and acts before you think. Blood may automatically drain from the skin to feed the muscles and brain, the heart beats faster to increase circulation and provide oxygen, adrenaline is released, etc. But the body acts without a controller. Later, you might say, 'I am in danger,' and you feel fear. But the body feels no fear. There is only action. Fear is a psychological reaction, based on memory. Psychological survival is an illusion. Distinguish between biological and psychological activity.

Q. Is it the same with anger, jealousy, hate, and so on?
A. They are all concepts. Once you understand the principle, you can transpose it to every dimension of life. When you feel anger, don't judge it or name it. Make it an object of perception free from the interference of the intellect. Thoughts may come and go but if you give them no hold, you come to no conclusion. Sustain looking without conclusion and you'll feel space between you and what you call anger. This space is not a psychological feeling but a genuine global body sensation. The more you become interested in the real anger, the more objective it becomes, a perception you observe rather than an emotivity you are lost in. You will see it is only fixed energy with none of the qualities the mind calls anger.

Q. What if the emotion emerges suddenly and uncontrollably?
A. When the crisis is over you must recollect in tranquil-

lity. Go back to the situation. Let it live again in your objective attention.

It is important that after every action you don't consider yourself as the doer. Say rather, 'There was a doing.' This witness state is a teaching principle, a crutch. It is a device to break the habit of identifying with thoughts and actions by creating a space relationship. But in fact the witness doesn't exist because in reality there is no such thing as memory or recalling. What you label the past is a present thought. Thought is always in the now, in present, conscious awareness. When the idea of being somebody disappears, the need for a witness disappears too.

Q. Is it possible to be completely free from all tension?
A. When you no longer conceptualise your sensations you will become more sensitive to contractions the moment they arise, before they are named. As you become more familiar with tension-free living, you will feel contraction in its subtlest movement. It is the same with thoughts. Before the thought, there is a pulsation. If you are very alert and sensitive you'll feel the pulsation the moment before it strikes the brain and becomes concretised.

When you live in freedom, tension still comes up where it belongs to biological survival, but it doesn't create compensation. It doesn't become part of the chain of reaction. The tension is felt but not fixed. Tension has a different shape when it is part of one's totality.

Q. I feel incredibly lonely all the time and hold onto relationships simply because they are better than nothing.
A. Who is alone? Don't be in a hurry to answer. Who is alone?

Q. Myself.
A. Is this 'myself' there when you aren't thinking about

it? As long as you take yourself to be somebody, you will feel isolation. The only difference between you and others is that they are taken by activity and their surroundings and you are taken by your absence of surroundings. In both cases there is identification with the object. It is exactly the same.

The next time you feel lonely ask: who is lonely? Look for this 'who'. You will never find it. When you feel lack, it is God-given. It is the biggest opportunity you can have in your life. You may not feel it so, but if you never felt lack you would never be drawn to inquire.

Q. I feel burdened by a sense of guilt that weighs on me.
A. As long as you believe in the self-image, there is guilt. See that this image is only a projection in space and time. You are not the film, you are the light that allows you to see the film. Free yourself from thinking you are the film. The film is fraction and fraction can only see fraction. Therefore, a fraction is conflict. As long as you don't live the whole, there is conflict. Live in emptiness, free from images, and you will come to feel fullness. While there is objectification you cannot live in fullness. It is beautiful to live in nothingness, to be nothing. To live in emptiness means to live free of all images, free from all points of view, free even of the idea of nothingness. I suggest you read Meister Eckhart's sermon, 'Blessed are the Poor', which says more beautifully than I could ever say what real emptiness, real poverty, is.

Q. Do emotions and feelings still come up when you live in emptiness?
A. Emotion, as you understand it, is an emotional state, what I call emotivity. It is reaction; it binds you to the I-image through memory and habit. Emotivity is repetition, as when you feel that you have felt a certain way

before. It springs from the desire for security. It is a movement of taking. Many people live in a continual emotivity without ever having questioned it.

Emotions, on the other hand, are always new. They are flexible. Emotion belongs to emptiness. It dissolves the ego. In emotion the subject-object duality is eliminated. It is beauty. When you are free of states and images and you see a piece of sculpture, a painting, or hear music, or read a poem, or watch the setting sun, or touch your beloved, there is no doer. There is only seeing, hearing, touching. In this freedom from ownership emotion comes up. It comes out of your own beauty. Emotion integrates but emotivity isolates. So free yourself from affectivity. In this absence of emotivity, you may have the impression at first that you become indifferent. But very soon you'll see that there is really affection for your surroundings. Emotion, affection, is giving.

Q. Do you agree that life is suffering?
A. When you are identified with existence, living in the chain of reaction, cause and effect, then life is suffering. But when for one moment you are completely out of this identification then suffering appears differently. It appears then because you have tasted freedom but are not completely attuned to it. In this suffering there is life. It is the great doubt that makes you dissatisfied with anything less than the whole. It brings you confirmation of what you are. Other suffering only leads to bankruptcy!

Q. How can I go beyond daily suffering?
A. The original cause of suffering is a feeling of isolation, of not being related to the whole. This brings conflict in your life. Generally you only see the conflict, the superficial suffering, but when suffering is contemplated deeply

beyond the level of the conflict, the root cause comes up. You must face the origins of suffering and not be distracted by secondary effects. It is the ego which suffers. When the fractional sufferer disappears then suffering points to oneness.

Q. Does the enlightened one suffer?
A. If there is any suffering it is in an unknown place where you feel others are not with you in freedom. But still your freedom radiates.

Q. Does one deal with physical pain in the same way as other sensations?
A. Yes. The body is fundamentally healthy. It has an organic memory of health. When the body is hurt there is a certain sensation but your reaction and memory exaggerate and maintain it. In looking at the sensation free from compensation and the interference of images, it will be greatly reduced. Most so-called pain is non-acceptance.

The work of a doctor is only to help the body find its own health. One must go with the organ, with the organic memory, not against it. Today, most medicine is involved in 'fighting' disease!

Q. How important is good nutrition?
A. Your body is what you think, feel and eat. Food is not only what you take in through the mouth. Your body is composed of the five elements – water, earth, air, fire, ether – and so your whole environment is food. How you handle the five elements constitutes good eating. Concerning what you absorb through the mouth, there is food which helps maintain the organism and there is so-called food to seduce the taste. What you eat is determined by your observation. Take note how it acts in you,

how you feel before and after a meal, how the body goes to sleep and wakes up. The body itself will bring you to a choice.

Q. What kind of exercise does the body need? I ask because I hear you teach a form of yoga based on the ancient Kashmir tradition.

A. Firstly, you will never hear me use the word 'yoga' to describe what I teach. Generally, yoga is understood in dualistic terms as the uniting of the supposed individual self with the supposed universal Self. It has thus become a process of attaining and becoming, a process of will. Although we use the traditional *asanas* and *pranayama*, postures and breathing techniques, codified by Patanjali, the work begins with the conviction that there's nothing to achieve or become. It is only a way to be acquainted with what we take for granted as body, senses and mind. It brings us to know first what we are not, and eventually what we fundamentally are becomes clear. Then body, senses and mind are an expression of our wholeness.

When I was travelling in India in 1968 I happened to meet a saintly man and his disciples. I was drawn to them by their beautiful singing and performing of certain ritual actions, *pujas*. In the course of conversation with this man, I asked what he understood by the word yoga and was struck by the simplicity of his answer. He said, 'Yoga is right sitting, right doing, right behaviour in the moment itself. It is being appropriate to the situation in all your mental and physical action. Yoga is being united with the present.'

Q. How can we come to this right sitting, right behaviour? What do you mean exactly by becoming acquainted with what we are not?
A. The body is the five senses and the five senses are the

71

body, but generally the five senses are conditioned. For you the body is more or less an image built up in your brain, so it is not the real body which wakes up in the morning but a series of images that come to you. What is the point of exercising the conditioned body? All you do is reinforce its patterns. When the five senses are freed from memory, it will be felt that the body is mainly layers of sensation. Encouraging body feeling gives you a foretaste of your global feeling. It also brings you back to the balance of your whole body.

Global feeling goes beyond the physical shape of the body. It flows into the surrounding space. It is this feeling of expansion that helps in annihilating the I-image since the ego is only a contraction, a fraction. Expansion is the ego-less 'non-state'. In expansion there is no isolation. It is love.

Q. What is the tool one uses in this approach?
A. It is a profound 'listening', free from mental interference. Through this listening the paralysed subtle layers of energy of the body can unfold. In working through listening free from will or attainment, the body finds its original state of lightness, expansion, transparency and the natural harmonisation of energy. In working with the expanded body one comes to the expanded mind. The expanded body-mind is the threshold of our real being, objectless awareness. Although in the beginning the emphasis may seem to be on the body, in the end the emphasis is on listening itself, which is receptivity, openness, our real nature in which body and mind exist.

Q. What do you mean by 'body-feeling'?
A. What you call your body is only an envelope in which lives a subtle body. This inner body is subtle energy, the life-force which supports the physical body. All our sensi-

tivity depends on this life-force. Paradoxically, although the subtle body resides in the physical body it radiates beyond it and encounters the surroundings. So the body in its wholeness has a much greater extension than is generally realised. As the physical body throughout life grows increasingly conditioned by striving it becomes a knot of tensions and contractions and the subtle body is paralysed in its expression. Its radiation is hindered and the physical body is isolated from its environment. When this life-force is obstructed there is a premature ageing of the physical body which manifests first as a diminution of sensitivity and energy. In the natural healthy body each cell is penetrated by life.

Our approach is therefore to bring the energy body back to its full expression as it is in infancy. In being aware of it, it comes to complete functioning. Thus, the first thing we do in our bodywork is to awaken the energy body, to make it an object of awareness. This energy is felt, it is a sensation. It is this that I call body-feeling. When the sensation of energy is fully alive it brings about a modification of the physical structure. Any other attempt to alter the body comes from will, the mind, and is violence. In any movement it is the energy body, the vital body, which moves and takes the physical body with it. The emphasis in our teaching on this level is therefore not on the posture or physical structure but on this body-feeling. When the vital body is awakened, all the muscle structure is relaxed and a reorchestration of energy takes place.

Each sense is no longer limited to its physical organ but expands to the whole body. In this global sensation all the senses participate. Being in expansion automatically takes you beyond the idea of being a separate entity. The body-work is one way to bring you to oneness with all beings.

Q. What happens to the energy body at the death of the physical body?
A. It dissolves into universal energy.

Q. Is the astral body the same as the energy body? When we dream, which body travels?
A. The astral body belongs to the psyche, the energy body to the senses. The astral body is even more subtle energy. In dreaming it is the astral body which takes the energy body with it for its expression. But thinking about the astral body is an escape from the real question, Who am I? Don't be seduced by states. Your real nature is not a state.

Q. I feel I understand what you say but later I act from the individual point of view. Is it just a question of waiting for clarity?
A. Act in daily life according to your understanding. This is very important. Take note afterwards whether you have acted in a mechanical way. After you have noticed several times that you have reacted in a certain way, you will begin to catch yourself in the middle of the reaction and a time will come, you can be sure, when you are alert before you react. So don't qualify your doing or condemn yourself. It's enough just to see it. When you've seen it you have taken the charcoal out of the fire. You have removed the fixed energy that holds your pattern. In simply being alert and welcoming, you are already living in your fullness.

Q. How can I recognise a maturing in my way of living?
A. You will feel increasingly free from antagonism and contradiction. If you feel a contradiction in your daily life and you remain stuck in it, you can call it a lack of maturity. But crisis is a beautiful thing when it leaves

you without reference unable to move to the left or the right. You feel that all you have done in life is useless, that nothing can happen. It brings you to despair. Then you really have to face it. In facing it you come to waiting in openness. In other words, the crisis will no longer be emphasised but the way of facing it will become important. You live in the unmoving itself.

This is a new level of understanding, a jump in maturity. It is only when this switchover from the object, the situation, to the subject, the welcoming of it, occurs that real maturity is possible. Maturity does not come through accumulation of learning, experiences, systems, ideas, concepts. It comes when you cannot walk and have to leap. All your being is struck in this leap and clarity arises.

There may be many such leaps but you do not need many, maybe only one!

Q. How is it that I feel the disturbance of thoughts and feelings even more though I feel much more deeply orientated than before?
A. If you throw a rock into a stormy lake, though there would be waves you could not see them. But throw a pebble into a calm lake and you will see all the ripples clearly.

Q. I feel in a kind of limbo because I know I am not the object and am not interested in exploring it further, yet I feel I must continue to explore in some way or else the fire of the quest will die out!
A. This feeling of helplessness where you don't move in any direction comes when the object has lost its flavour. If you really live this moment you will find yourself in a new dimension where the emphasis is more on the quietness in the action rather than the activity itself. Joy then

lies in being 'behind' the action rather than immersed in it. But of course, as I say very often, this 'behind feeling' is not an accurate phrase because it implies an attitude of detached observation which is not what is meant at all. Detachment is a mental activity, whereas in the stillness in the midst of activity there is no place for a psychological gap.

It is vital that you live according to your understanding. Once you have seen the patterns, remain alert and do not go in them.

Q. There was a time when I felt that I was without thought, without body, without head. Why does this state not last?

A. This observing in the absence of thoughts is still a mind function albeit of the most subtle form. The reflex to identify with phenomena remains. The non-state which is your real nature has nothing to do with the absence or presence of phenomena.

Q. I was once in the non-state you speak of. How can it be permanent? I find I try to repeat the circumstances which led to it.

A. When you have once had the non-experience you can have it now, but it has nothing to do with memory. You cannot repeat it. All you can do is be aware that there are moments in daily life when you are not experiencing, for example, when you are astonished, when a desire is obtained, when an action is accomplished or a thought comes to its end. Also, the moment before the body wakes up or goes to sleep. It is enough to know these moments and you will spontaneously be solicited by them.

It may happen that one is struck in all one's being unexpectedly. When the body-mind is not ready, it makes an experience of the non-experience. The ego, feeling a threat to its existence, makes a state of the moment. This is why the mind must be informed and the body ready. Otherwise you put the timeless moment into the frame of memory and then try to repeat it. Once you know your non-state, see only how you go back into the old patterns.

Q. So if one is not ready in mind and body it remains accidental. What does it mean, 'to be ready'?
A. You must be acquainted with the art of giving up on all levels. Receiving is knowingly giving up. It is important to come to surrender, to receiving, on the phenomenal level. This means the mind must know its limits and the body must be free from habitual patterns, contractions, tensions. It is an openness on all levels of the psycho-physiological structure. Then when the insight strikes you, it spontaneously saturates you. It finds no localisation.

Q. So there must be a profound desire, a willingness and an ability to completely let go. Otherwise residual patterns bring you back to the old ways, or one's activities in life may take you away.
A. The art of transposition must be explored. It calls for complete receptivity so that understanding is transposed into living. When you are familiar with this transposition, letting go, then when there is a sudden rectification on the phenomenal plane you do not contract away from it but let yourself be completely taken. Take the time to be completely permeated.

Q. Is the role of a teacher to help us in this letting go?
A. Yes. The teacher shows you how to come to a giving up, how to become an artisan in this transposition. But all teaching is for the mind. There must be no ambition, no intention to attain anything.

Q. So before the insight we call enlightenment it is important to be physically prepared, living in openness and deep psycho-physiological receptivity. Then the insight is spontaneously transposed to every arena of living. My question is why does intellectual clarity seem to precede right living for most people? Why is it we are unwilling to put our understanding into practice? I often think of St. Augustine's cry: 'Lord, give me chastity, but do not give it yet!'
A. Transposition is an art. One must be an artisan. The transposition of understanding into life gives insecurity to the person. In transposition there is a passage where there is no hold for an 'I' because it calls for inquiring, listening, being open. Most people prefer to remain in insecurity rather than let the ego completely die. The passage is painful for the residues of the person and most try to avoid it. Once the transposition is accomplished there is no more ego to worry.

Q. A practical question – is the body-work you teach to bring one to the art of letting go?
A. Yes – only this. In letting go there is expansion of mind and body and in this you have a fore-feeling of reality, your globality.

Q. You say often that we must become acquainted with dying. Is this the same as giving up or letting go? Don't you think that many people postpone this until the actual moment of death?
A. Yes. But then it is necessary to have someone awakened to assist you in this step of letting go. This is supposedly the priest's role in the last rites. How to die and how to sleep are the same. Before sleep you may come to a knowing giving up. It is the same with the dissolution of the born. You should be alert to the natural giving up

before going to sleep. First be familiar with this and then you come to be knowingly in letting go in the waking state. This is the real meaning of the word death. It is the real significance of the word sacrifice.

Q. In the morning there is sometimes a moment before the body wakes up when I feel already awake. Is this the awareness you speak of which is our nature behind all functioning?
A. Yes. This moment depends on the letting go before going to sleep we just spoke about.

Q. How can this brief moment become continuous?
A. When you don't lose yourself in activities you will find your whole morning grounded in it. You do the activities but you remain behind them. You are not glued to them. See in the instant it happens how you identify again with the body-mind as soon as it wakes up. Don't objectify the moment before the identification as an absence of activity. Your eternal being, consciousness, is the light behind all activity, all perception.

Q. As the moment before the body wakes up is dependent on the moment before it goes to sleep, is there a similar waking up without objects after the great sleep, death, if one lets go of all the residues of the individual person beforehand?
A. Yes. The objectless wakefulness after death, consciousness, is the same as that moment before the body wakes up in the morning. All appears in consciousness which is not affected by birth or death. There is not one moment without consciousness, so after the death of the body consciousness is there as always.

Q. So the one who has died to the person in life wakes

up in consciousness. What about everyone else?
A. Everything is in consciousness, but, as we said, one can be awake in consciousness or not. For most, after death, being consciousness is passive. The thing is to be knowingly consciousness: consciousness conscious of itself. This can only come about before the body dies. Since most people only know themselves as objects and do not know themselves as consciousness, few after death dissolve in consciousness which knows itself. Consciousness which knows itself is fulfilled and does not look for further expression.

Q. So the world as manifest is the expression of consciousness which does not yet know itself?
A. Exactly. Your true nature is to be knowingly consciousness. It is ultimate sufficiency.

Q. What you say has a beautiful ring to it. But how can you know these things if you have not yet witnessed the death of the body?
What proof can you give me that you really know what life after death is?
A. Consciousness, presence of life, is there before the body wakes up. It is prior to thought and thinking, It is what you are eternally. It is silent awareness, nameless, without attribute, but expressing itself in all names and forms. Many of the changes the body and vitality undergo as temporary expressions of consciousness are hypothetical. But there is nothing hypothetical about what you really are, which is continuous. Consciousness is its own proof, without object and without witness. When you live knowingly there is no death.

THE NATURE OF THINKING

Thinking is not based on thoughts.

Our real nature is stillness beyond all complementarities. It is presence without becoming. In the absence of becoming there is completeness and absolute tranquillity. This tranquillity is the home ground of all activity. The activity of thinking, like all activity, is grounded in wholeness. Tranquillity is the continuum in which thinking appears and disappears. What appears and disappears is in movement. It is energy extended in space and time. Thinking, energy, represents itself in discontinuity but as it arises out of and dies in stillness, fundamentally it is nothing other than this presence beyond past, present and future.

What we generally call 'thinking' is a process of memory. It is a projection built on the already known. All that exists, all that is perceived, is represented to the mind. Sequential thinking, rational or scientific thinking, thus begins with a fraction, a representation. Such fractional thinking is born from the conditioned idea that we are independent entities, 'selves', 'persons'. The notion of being a somebody conditions all other thinking because the person can only exist in the repetition of representation, the confirmation of the already known. The brain tends here toward constant representation. Memory is the originator of the idea of being a continuous entity. From the ultimate view thinking is a defence against the death of the ego. Who are you when you don't think? When you look away from thinking, where are you?

Thinking is generally an escape from your wholeness in which there is no one who thinks.

When the ingrained idea of a personal entity, a thinker, intender or doer, is absent, thinking still occurs as before in succession using memory but now this functioning is firmly rooted in the global background – wholeness, is-ness, non-duality. In the absence of a thinker, thinking is freed from all that is personal. There is no goal, motive, anticipation, intention, will or desire to conclude, etc. There is no psychological interference, no reference to a centre. Thinking freed from this memory comes out of the moment itself, is always new, always original. Think-ing does not here call forth the situation; the situation calls forth thinking and brings its own conclusion. All intentional, fragmentary movement must cease before the whole can operate. As long as there is movement in one direction, totality cannot find its own way. When scientific or rational thinking is grounded in presence it has a completely different outcome. It can never be monstrous.

Thinking freed from memory is truly creative. Every thought is an explosion to be manifested and an implosion to be reabsorbed into silence. The desire to be revealed and to be concealed is the Cosmic Dance, motiveless play for the joy of playing. True desire is nothing but this. All other desire is only a warping of, and an unconscious longing for, this ultimate desire. The essence of think-ing is this divine playing. Creative thinking never begins with the already known, a representation. It is born and dies in openness and merely uses functional memory for its expression. Where there is no thinker there is only a channel for the function of thinking. In this function-ing every representation is consciously grounded. When presence remains in thinking the name is not divorced from the form as it is in mechanical thinking which is conceptual and abstract. Creative 'thinking' is a jubilation of being.

In taking ourselves for separate entities we have forgotten our home ground and identified ourselves with an idea, a projection of individuality. It is not the endless expressions of silence that are the problem or cause complications, but our forgetting the source of all expression. This separation from our true nature brings us to false living. We do not allow expression to dissolve but crystallise it and then identify with – become lost in – this crystallisation.

Through this objectification, what we call 'the world' is created. We take existence for life itself. But life has no beginning and no end. Real living is playing, joy without object.

Q. How can I move from intentional thinking to creative thinking?
A. A mind grounded in stillness is always creative. It is always new, free from the past. It is naturally silent attention welcoming everything that comes up from the body, senses and imagination. Then there may be instantaneous appearings, spontaneous expressions in time and space of what we really are. All such expressions are a celebration on the plane of existence and a pointer to the home ground, stillness.

Only in our openness, our welcome nature that is not an attitude, can creativity occur. Welcoming alertness appears spontaneously when the idea of a centre of reference, someone who welcomes, who thinks, who likes and dislikes, is absent. The mind is then freed from the boundaries of successive thoughts and the senses, imagination and whole intelligence come into play in our unconditional attention. Since there's no controlling agent there can be no limitations of time and space and an appearance of simultaneity may occur. Later, of course, this global vision is realised in space and time. All great works of art appear in this way.

Q. Before creative thinking appears in space and time is there not a passage between the unknown and the formulation? The unknown seems to pass through archetypal symbols en route to expression.
A. Yes. These archetypes bridge the unknown and the universal known. They are not yet reduced to mere brain functions but have their dynamism in the totality.

Q. Is this realisation in space and time still spontaneous or does it belong to memory?
A. When you live in the background, consciousness, thinking appears as its expression in time and space, functional consciousness. It comes out of stillness but belongs to no one. There is no doer, only doing. So in consciousness, functional memory is used but there is no psychological involvement. When there is a spontaneous global insight, it leaves a kind of echo. For the artist this is the vision which is the continual background of his execution in space and time. By analogy, the truth-seeker lives from moment to moment with the echo of his real nature.

Q. You said that thought appears and disappears but my mind seems to be turning constantly.
A. Remember that the mind is only a vehicle. When we don't need our legs we don't use them. Likewise, let the mind rest when not needed. What we generally call thinking is either mechanical reaction to a projected outer stimulation or it is intentional and calculative. There is unconscious or conscious aggrandisement of the

self-image, psychological attainment. You see it already in very young children who dream of becoming. These dreams are born from and fed by society. In the present day everything turns around becoming. In becoming one is never present to the moment, the facts at hand. The 'I' goes back to the past and creates a future built on the already known. All becoming is one-dimensional, focused on the horizontal plane.

Q. Is not what you call divine play also becoming?
A. Divine play comes out of perfection. There is nothing to perfect, so strictly speaking it is not becoming because it never leaves wholeness. There is always presence. It is life playing with itself, expression for the joy of expressing. There is no agent. But in the becoming that we mostly know, presence is veiled. You have identified with the expression and not its source. You have made illusory what is fundamentally real. But there is nothing to try to change or give up. All you must do is identify with the source of the world, and not its playthings, the world of so-called objects.

Q. What does 'fundamentally real' mean?
A. That which exists in itself, has no need of an agent, is autonomous.

Q. Is this autonomous reality what you also call presence, stillness, the home ground, consciousness, etc.?
A. Yes. When you take away all perceptions, concepts and their agent, what remains? You can call it what you like, non-being or being, the ultimate subject, *sunyata*, *nirvana*. It is not an idea. It is stillness without anyone being still. It has nothing to do with the presence or absence of objects. Existence is in it and thus points to it, but it is not in existence.

Q. How can I switch over my identification with objects to an identification with that consciousness to which objects point?

A. See that existence is only because you are. But you have mistaken yourself for a subject, an independent entity. This subject is still an object, something that can be perceived. In reality there are no objects. These are mind-productions. See that you are identified with a mind-production. All that you try to understand comes through what is already known. Real understanding is being understanding and this appears suddenly when there is listening without conclusion. Do not concretise the symbol but let it unfold in your openness. Live with what it tells you from morning to evening and you will one day be taken by your wholeness. The perception points to your real nature. All so-called objects exist only to bring you back to what you are. Truth does not lie in words but in that to which they point, just as 'salt' is not salty.

Q. When you say truth is that to which words point, are you using the word truth to mean consciousness, stillness, our being, that which is fundamentally real as you said earlier?

A. There are many facts but there is one truth. Facts can be known by the mind as we know 2 + 2 = 4 or the sun is in the sky. But the ordinary mind can never understand more than simply facts. The smaller can never comprehend the larger. Because the less belongs to the more, the mind may carry a fore-feeling of the whole but it is only when it sees its limits and relaxes its grasp on the appearing of phenomena that what is beyond the accumulation of knowable facts, the all-possible, can appear. When the mind releases its control the whole body is a welcoming organ. Then what appears is globally felt, not limited by thought. Truth is not in the realm of having knowledge but is knowing as being. It is the direct perception of the intrinsic nature of all existence.

It is a degeneration of the word truth to use it in the sense of fact. Facts can be proved but there is no argument for truth. It is its own proof. All that is perceived is an expression of truth. Everything is grounded in truth and if we do not know truth we cannot know its expression. Nothing is autonomous, and in this sense real, except truth. Untruth is all that has no autonomous being, which depends on a knower to be known. If the knower knows itself in truth, in consciousness, then all perception is spontaneously grounded in consciousness too.

Q. You often say there is only one thought possible at a time, and that consciousness and its object are one. Would you clarify this?
A. Our brains normally function in such a way that at a given moment there is only one thought at a time. You can never have two thoughts or perceptions simultaneously. You might say you can, for example, cook a meal and think about how hungry you are at the same time. Of course there are thousands of motor reflexes going on in us all at one time, but you cannot be consciously with two thoughts or actions at once. The succession is very rapid but apparent simultaneity is just memory. An object and subject, cause and effect, cannot exist at the same moment. Past, present and future, space and time, are also memory. In daily life there is apparent duality because this is how the brain functions, but all functioning appears in non-duality.

However, there are exceptional moments when we go beyond ordinary thinking. There may be flashes of the timeless simultaneity that is our real being. Great artists and scientists are familiar with these moments, moments when the reflex of the ego is in abeyance and the brain is spontaneously integrated in global intelligence.

Q. You say that our natural state, consciousness, is behind all function. You also said that in daily life duality appears in non-dual being. Is there another level of consciousness which we use in everyday activity?
A. Consciousness simply is. There is no point of reference, so how can there be levels? Be clear that what is generally called consciousness is related to something: 'consciousness of'. 'Consciousness of' is functional consciousness. It belongs to the moment only and as it is an extension of pure consciousness is always perfectly appropriate. What we call pure consciousness is impossible for our modern psychology to grasp. For psychology, the interval between two thoughts or two states is an absence. But when you speak of an absence, there is a knower of the absence. The knower is consciousness. So consciousness is continuity. All that is perceived appears and disappears in consciousness, is an expression, a prolongation of consciousness.

Q. How can I come to know consciousness free from relation to things?
A. Become more aware of the moment a thought or activity comes to an end. Live in identity with this moment. You will feel the ego looking for a new thought to continue its existence. It cannot survive without the fuel of subject-object relation. When you are free of the self-image, your thinking is only an occasional vehicle. When there is nothing to think, you don't think. Continual thinking is a defence, a fortress for the ego, nothing else. Become familiar in daily life with looking at situations without the intervention of the 'I' and its desires, aversions, resistances, preferences, etc. Sustain this motiveless looking

and you will find that when the observer and observed are no longer fuelled, they disappear. You will then be in looking itself. This simple looking, free from the doer and the done, is the timeless consciousness, the background of all activities.

Q. I'm aware of moments in daily life without activity. But afterwards I lose these moments.
A. You are accustomed in daily life to emphasise the object part and so, in the absence of objects, the reflex to objectify brings you to emphasise the absence of perception out of habit. You still remain bound to the object, the perception. Let us take an analogy: You have lived for many years in a room with a picture hanging on a wall. One day you take it down to be cleaned. Now, each time you go into the room, what hinders you from seeing the wall in itself? It is the absence of the picture. But you can only know the absence because you are present. The absence refers to your presence. So explore what is behind the absence.

Q. It seems to call for tremendous alertness to sustain the looking and exploration and not to be taken by secondary factors like feelings, states and thoughts.
A. Yes, but there is no effort in being alert, Accept that the natural state of the brain is attention, alertness, and relax in this acceptance. It will bring you to a new dimension.

Be like wild animals who are perfectly alert without reference to any self-image, past or future. The natural body is as awake as a panther. Alertness is not a doing, it is a receiving.

Q. Will you clarify the difference between being and existence?

A. Being, pure consciousness, is not in the categories of time and space any more than we can speak of infinity in terms of in and out. Existence is consciousness objectifying itself without cause or reason. It is energy dispersed or actualised in space and time. We could say functional consciousness is the link between being and existence. It is energy in repose, potential energy.

Your real nature is prior to all function. You are the light that makes function possible. Be this light. All that exists is in you. Nothing is outside. When you sit here the ground is affected in China, Paris and Benares. You are war and you are peace.

Q. What is the relation between thought and existence?
A. Existence is before you name it, think it. It is called up from moment to moment when you perceive it. All that is perceived is existence. If there were no perceiver there would be no existence.

Q. Is this not philosophical Idealism?
A. Not at all. The perceived is in the perceiving but the perceiving is not in the perceived. The perceiver is not a fraction, mind, but totality. Thus the perceived is already potentially in the perceiver, the whole. It is not that there is no existence. It is simply that what we name existence is not pure existence because existence is within the whole being. Unless we live this we cannot know existence. Because physics emphasises the perceived, the part, and not the perceiver, the whole, it cannot fully understand the nature of existence. Pure existence is created in your silence and dies in your silence at each moment. What you call a permanent existence, the creation, is a thought, a convention, a gentlemen's agreement.

Q. What would bring one to become interested in the

THE NATURE OF THINKING

global perceiver rather than the perceived?

A. When you know that creation is not permanent and that all is born and dies at every moment in your presence, you may be drawn to inquire into this presence. You may know the science of all brain function but you will never know the perceiver. You may regress ad infinitum intellectually through a series of subjects but you can never know the ultimate subject objectively. Oppenheimer said that the scientist could never come to know totality because he can never know the knower scientifically. Consciousness cannot he objectified. Love, compassion and humour are not analysable. Physics will never be able to understand enlightenment. It will always remain a mystery to the analytical brain. When you put lovers' tears under a microscope you can analyse them but you can never say where they come from.

The first step, therefore, is to come to the conviction that objective knowing is limited. Then the mind comes to a stop and you cross over from exploring the object to exploring the subject aspect. However, since there is still the tendency, the reflex to make this aspect an attitude, an object, the proof only comes when you abide in non-objectifying and are suddenly taken by presence without object.

Q. Is this crossing over from interest in the object to the subject, the question 'Who am I?'
A. Yes. The question can be asked on many levels. But the real question comes in the giving up of asking on the levels of body, senses and mind. You may know the story of King Janaka and his guru. They had been discussing the dreaming and waking states and Vasishtha had told the King that they were the same. That night Janaka dreamed he was a beggar and in the morning he excitedly asked his guru, 'I dreamed I was a beggar.

Am I a beggar who is dreaming he is Janaka or Janaka who is dreaming he is a beggar?' Vasishtha replied, 'You are neither. You are the Self.' Then King Janaka clearly understood and joyfully exclaimed, 'Ah! I am the Self!' But Vasishtha said, 'That is the last hindrance. In thinking it you cannot be it.'

Q. Would you elaborate further on the difference between knowledge and knowing as being?
A. All that we know has a reference point. It is known through other things, by comparison. If you have never tasted jicama root I might describe it to you as a combination of an apple and raw potato. From this you would come to know it to some degree. But there is nothing to compare to your real nature. It is not something you can know as you know other things. It can only be knowing. Thus, every step made to come near takes us away from it. We are in stillness, our real nature, when there is no movement in any direction.

The sun needs no light to shine but the moon is dependent on the sun for its light. Likewise, all knowledge has its source in being knowledge.

Q. In order for mind to feel its limits must thoughts come to a standstill?
A. The organic nature of the mind is movement, spontaneous function. This belongs to reality. In geometrical terms we can say that reality is behind the mind. Never try to stop thoughts. Your real nature, stillness, is not in the absence of thought but is the source of thought and no-thought. All techniques to stop the mind are part of becoming, achieving, the mind itself. Simply take note of those times when thought comes to an end. Give these moments more emphasis. When allowed to do so, the mind will automatically fall into correct functioning,

acting and resting when appropriate. The body is fundamentally healthy with an organic memory. If we don't tamper with it, it takes itself in charge.

When there is nothing to be done, when no situation calls for functional memory and psychological memory is in abeyance, then one is in stillness free from past, present and future. This stillness is autonomous of all memory, individual or collective. It is the source of activity. Creative thinking can only come out of this background without the impediment of the ego.

Q. Why is my mind in constant movement?
A. Because you are identified with movement. If it stopped where would you find yourself? You must explore the fleeting intervals between thoughts and that moment before the body wakes up in the morning.

Q. So this continual agitation keeps my feeling of being alive?
A. When you take yourself for a person you are dependent on thoughts, situations, events, movement to keep the person alive. The person must be allowed to die. Become accustomed to dying, and you will know what life really is!

Q. Is there any value in techniques to quiet the continual agitation of the mind?
A. A controlled mind can never be free. It becomes a rigid tool without subtlety. A disciplined mind can never bring about the dying of the illusory self-image. You can never come to the new by pursuing the old. The mind can never transmute itself. It can bring about changes on the cerebral level but you remain in the psychological frame with an 'I', however subtle, at the centre.

Why waste energy with what you are not? Go straight to what you are. Our real nature is closer than

WHO AM I?

all thought. It is the source of all thought. The mind cannot grow towards what it already is. In the business of technique and discipline you look for a result. You are always projecting the known and though you may come to some new chemical transformation of the body, some new or subtle emotional state, you cannot come to the natural state of being. Understand that though technique is necessary for learning a skill like a language or the piano, you cannot come to what you are through mind-effort. In techniques you go away from your real nature. The mind is a useful tool for accumulative learning, but it is only one part of human life. When it asks 'Who am I?' it eventually realises its limitations and surrenders to its source. This leads you from knowing things to being the knowing itself.

Q. Is there a recognisable point at which the mind knows its limits and surrenders to being knowledge?
A. When there is scientific inquiry without judgement or conclusion, all the elements of the situation are welcomed. Generally our choices, our likes and dislikes prevent us from seeing all the elements. In naked observation the situation can unfold in all its aspects. When the desire to come to a conclusion has dissolved and attention, alertness, is sustained, at a certain point it is like a magnet which suddenly attracts all the elements to itself. There is a momentary representation that encompasses the whole situation.

This is the last function of the intellect which does not concretise this representation, and it is suddenly absorbed in being understanding. Action appears spontaneously. Every situation contains its own conclusion when the mind does not impose one.

Q. Why do you stimulate the mind in your teaching if it

cannot bring us to knowing ourselves?
A. It brings you to question life. It helps you to find the perspective. You cannot stop the intellectual capacities once they have been set in motion. They must come to a natural end. The mind must come to a representation that it is only a function. This is the clarity of the mind. Until the intellect clearly feels its limits it must explore itself. When we cannot find something precious we will not be satisfied until we have looked under every stone. But there comes a moment when every stone in life is overturned and we still have not found what we are looking for. Then we are brought to a stop. The dynamism to search is halted. This quietness has nothing to do with the mind. It is the arena of knowing as being without objects. It is the support of all activity and non-activity.

Do you know the story told by the Sufi saint Mulla Nasruddin? I adapt it a little at each telling!

Mulla was crossing a street in his village when a man approached him saying, 'Do you know that your wife is being unfaithful to you?' Mulla quickly replied, 'That's impossible. My wife would never be unfaithful to me.' The man answered, 'I can prove it to you At midnight tonight she has a rendezvous with her lover under the fig tree at the edge of the village.' Mulla was very upset and, anticipating a duel with his wife's lover, went to buy a pistol.

All day he practised and thought about the fight and at eleven in the evening he went to the fig tree in a terrific state of mind. He climbed into the tree and, being a very passionate man, leapt from branch to branch in a frenzy of jealousy and anger. He pictured his wife in her lover's arms and practised from every angle the blow he would deliver his rival. At ten minutes to twelve he listened carefully but could not yet hear anything. At five to twelve he was in a state of unbearable agitation and

95

expectation. At three minutes to twelve there was still no sound of them and every nerve in his body was on edge. At twelve o'clock he was as unmoving as a tiger about to pounce on its prey. But still nothing happened under the tree. Then he was suddenly struck in all his being by a tremendous insight: 'I'm not married!'

Q. That's a great story! It seems that he went literally out of his mind, beyond his mind. But what was his mental state when the insight struck? Perhaps if I understand that I won't have to go quite so far as Mulla did!
A. Until twelve o'clock he was concentrated on the object, the representation of the scene. Then there came a moment when the mind found no more hold and the representation disappeared. He was no longer in the mind. The outer situation no longer fuelled further activity. The mind must come to exhaustion. When it gives up we are taken by our real nature. But the twelfth hour of the mind can be at any moment.

Q. What is the significance of the man in the story?
A. The man takes Mulla for married and Mulla accepts this unquestioningly. The man is society which takes you for the body-mind. 'Everyman' is second-hand information, hearsay, the taken-for-granted, so-called common sense.

Q. How can we see a situation clearly without the critical mind?
A. You can only see a situation when fractional looking, the point of view, is dissolved. When looking from a particular stance you narrow the field of vision through pre-selection. When you face a situation in openness without any intention or motive, it unfolds all the elements of its story and, as we said, at a certain point these appear

as a whole which then spontaneously vanishes in a conclusion, an action. It happens organically. There is no need of a person who makes choices or concludes. When the tiger spots his prey, he knows in a moment his own capacities and the distance, health, strength and speed of the animal, and in a second integrates this into action – stalking, running, waiting, letting it go. In non-directed awareness there is no longer thinking in the usual sense of the word. There is only creative thinking, spontaneous thinking and action.

You are like a white sheet of blotting paper. When everything has been absorbed, in alertness without choice, then understanding appears. It comes without volition. What is free from all volition is a gift. We feel understanding as an offering. Action which comes from understanding never leaves a residue. The mind has a natural function but we let it dictate to all the senses.

Q. Is it the same as in the Zen art of archery, where thinking impedes action?
A. Exactly. In the art of archery the important thing is to look away from the target, that is, to free yourself from the will of attaining. When you are free from the desire to achieve, you feel yourself in oneness and the target is one with you. In open attention the target is brought into awareness. When there is someone trying to do something there is separation. But free from intention, all the muscles and bone structure relax and what remains is pure energy ready for use. In archery the arrow shoots itself when there is no person prevailing. The position of alertness appears naturally in letting go. What is called beginner's luck is the freedom of the beginner from ideas of himself.

Q. So success is not due to one-pointedness as is often thought?

A. No, not one-pointedness in the sense of concentration. Concentration is a relationship with the particular and attention is a relationship with the whole. Concentration is a resistance to and a contraction away from the multidimensionality of attention. Without resistance your natural alertness burns like a flame. The words 'one' and 'pointedness' are not really marriageable!

Q. Can we have a geometrical representation of our whole life as well as of a specific situation?
A. Absolutely. It is important that the intellect becomes clear and orientated. Otherwise experience is accidental. When the linear mind is relaxed, a spatial representation of all the elements of life may appear in multidimensional attention. This is the ultimate representation. It is not a representation of the ultimate. In specific circumstances the intellect sees the whole situation and joyfully dissolves in spontaneous action which comes from the situation itself. In seeing all the circumstances of life the intellect gratefully abdicates its global insight to dissolve in knowing as being.

Q. When the mind comes to a spatial representation is its nature changed?
A. A global insight orientates the mind and energy from its habitual dispersion. This is the only way we can use the expression 'one-pointed'. It happens spontaneously. There is no effort, no will, no concentration involved. Nor is it introverted, which is a psychological category and means contraction from the whole. A transitional period of introspection may occur as one is taken by the exploration of this orientation.

Q. Do you think the global representation of all the elements of one's life situation is what the Buddha meant

THE NATURE OF THINKING

when he said he saw all his past lives in the moment before enlightenment?
A. What we call psychological memory is the content of your past. When the contents are seen from your wholeness, that is, when there is no particular centre of reference, they appear as clear objective facts. Then instantaneously there is a transference of energy and psychological memory is dissolved. All residues of guilt, regret and unintegrated sensations like pleasure or pain disappear and one is taken by what is, when nothing remains.

Q. The global geometrical representation is still a duality, a perception. How is it possible that one gives up even this most subtle relationship?
A. The informed mind knows that knowledge is not fully accomplished and it is ready to let go. At this point the duality of observer and observed is so transparent that the oneness of consciousness overcomes it. You cannot go by will over the threshold. You are taken.

When one takes a progressive path it is virtually impossible to be released from the subtle hold of duality. The reflex to identify with thought has been ingrained through training. But in the direct way the intellect is constantly grounded in the non-dual background. You live with it at every moment. From the beginning the mind knows it is limited and lives in welcoming a new dimension. The intellect has not been conditioned and its fluidity is vitally important for this last discernment. The intellect remembers what you have heard and hitherto have taken as a possibility – that you are not experience. From believing it is limited, it experiences the limits. This remembering brings the moment of grace and you are taken in your wholeness.

You must come to the lively conclusion that an object exists because you are. It appears in you because it is

only a projection of energy in space and time, and it is
consumed in you.

Q. How does transmutation take place in stillness?
A. In being left to silence the mind undergoes a transformation. It is no longer a restless, self-centred instrument rationalising and justifying mechanical behaviour.
In stillness the intellect is illumined. Transmutation
touches every corner of your being, all its obscure urges,
and a new human being is born. Knowing as being is
not an idea. An idea has no dynamic force. Understanding as being comes through direct perception, perception
without a perceiver. If we allow dynamic perception to
operate, it eliminates disorder and the habit of twisting
the process of perception to our wishes, ambitions, habits, expectations, desires, and so on.

Intelligence is not conditioned or inherited. It is not
contaminated by memory. It is not related to somebody,
to any cerebral function. It lies in the complete relaxation of the psycho-physical structure when an unknown
quantity of sensitivity which is not generated by the
brain begins to operate. It is a motion permeating the
whole being and taking place in the whole universe.

Q. Earlier, you talked about creative thinking which
springs from the unknown. Would you talk now about
scientific or rational thought?
A. Rational thinking is a vehicle for maintaining our
biological existence in daily life. It moves in the already
known, what has been agreed on as an individual or collective convention. It is functional memory for organising
energy into useful patterns of thought. Rational, logical or
scientific thinking starts from the known, thought derives
from thought, but when it claims no authorship, never
says 'I know' or 'I have done', then it refers to its home

THE NATURE OF THINKING

ground. When there is no psychological involvement, it is an expression of silence in time and space. The background of rational thinking is that non-representational presence we can call silent contemplation. However, the function of rational thinking is only a fraction of life. It should not be allowed to obscure the depths of our being. Unfortunately, like all our functions, rational thinking more often than not loses its purity and becomes directed by intention. Most so-called rational or technological thinking today is calculative. In calculative thinking is the desire of the individual to achieve a result. Intentional thinking is based on accumulation of definition and conclusion, the past, the already known. Unhappily for the world, almost all scientific and supposedly artistic thinking today is calculative, the urge to achieve.

There is a psychological goal hidden in the functional aim. Thought here is divorced from its home ground and identified with the person, the controller, the centre of reference. All desire to achieve is still within the self-centred field which binds us to a result. It is very difficult for people to understand that perfect function only emerges in the complete absence of end-gaining.

Q. You said that when the question 'Who am I?' comes up the inquiry moves in a different way than that to which we are accustomed. Would you say more about the nature of inquiry into one's true being?
A. The intellect that is used to inquire 'Who am I?' is the intellect that functions spontaneously free from the I-image. Only in this freedom can real questions emerge. Thus true inquiry appears when thinking is left in its home ground, before it becomes representational. Inquiry is before the urge to objectify. It is forethought. Meditative thinking is looking away from thinking. It is a tool, a statement of facts without any relation to a sup-

posed person. It is the release of all grasping and will-
ing. Inquiry never dominates, manipulates or defines. It
is free of interpretation. It is an open-ended question, a
question that is lived and explored in its question-nature
and is not driven to a close. What you fundamentally are
has no beginning and no conclusion. Why then look for
conclusions? Inquiry is attention, welcoming all upcoming. This brings us to the art of listening, to our primal
awareness.

Q. Then what you call 'listening' is fundamental in
inquiry?
A. Yes. Listening is an alert receptivity to all upcoming. It is passive only in that it is free from any hint of
someone who listens. When judgement, criticism, comparison, valuation are no longer controlling the psychosomatic structure, the whole body spontaneously comes
into listening. It is important to realise that it is not an
attitude. In the emptiness of striving and the desire to
achieve, presence is found. But at first you may make
this non-striving a state, an absence. Very often we live
in the absence of striving without exploring it. This is a
precarious position, life without flavour, a wasteland, the
dark night of the soul. But inquire into the real nature
of this 'absence' and you will discover presence in the
absence of all becoming. Never try to visualise the stillness or objectify the emptiness. Dare to live sometimes
in the beauty of Silence and you will feel how all logic
and understanding take shape in it, in yourself. Then
there comes a moment when you are being understanding. In this instant there is no knowing that is not awareness. All residues of objectivity are burned and there is
no more memory.

You can only be reality. You can never know it. But
as the known appears and disappears in this reality, it

belongs to it. It is the known which ultimately reveals the unknown. There is no hierarchy of reality. All is real.

Q. How can you say in the same breath that you can never know reality and that the known reveals the unknown? *A.* We are limited by vocabulary. The words must be heard with a certain flexibility just as you gladly give a poet poetic licence. Always listen to the whole context of the answer and how it acts in you. Do not isolate yourself from the symbolic power of words by taking them out of the global background.

Q. What is the origin of thought and word? *A.* A thought, a word, is a sound born out of soundlessness. Sound and silence are interrelated. You cannot hear a sound without hearing silence. Explore this silence. See how sound is born out of it. Sounds born from silence are powerful and can penetrate. Sound is vibration, movement, energy, thought and action. Thus, all sound not knowingly related to silence has no dynamism, no power to penetrate darkness and ignorance.

Q. I often find myself saying the wrong thing at the wrong time. How can I come to 'right speech'? *A.* In right speech there is no psychological involvement. Language, speaking, thinking, that are free from the ego, are complete in themselves, autonomous and spontaneous. Right speech makes no comparisons and does not refer to a speaker. It is purely factual. Attention is a spontaneous action of the brain and it recognises forms and names them. Psychological language on the other hand is always a qualification. It either refers to a centre or makes comparison between objects. For example, you may be taken by the beauty of a painting. But you may also feel the reflex to interpret it, own it, and so on. Take note of these reflexes that interfere with pure observation. When personal thinking comes in, you are no longer open to beauty.

Use words, thinking, in a right way. In using them in a right way you come to clarity. As long as you live on the plane of believing you are an individual entity, you fix the words on the level of this experience and their symbolic function as pointers to stillness is not realised. Real apperception can only take place in the complete annihilation of the pseudo-entity. When you speak and listen from your wholeness without evaluation and comparison, then the words are not fixed and dissolve in this completeness.

Q. Are you saying that language as we generally use it does not point to our real nature?
A. In daily life today language is concentrated on the verbal and as such is used for reference between so-called objects. Words are terms recollected on the level of experience and memory. In the world language functions in space and time. But the world is not an objective, autonomous reality. Our habitual way of using language is too limited. The real function of words is to act as pointers to the silence from which they spring.

Words are windows from emptiness to emptiness. They are the frame, the threshold. A word is like a bird which, crossing the threshold, becomes visible for a moment and we can glimpse its glorious feathers. If we follow it as it disappears it leads us to emptiness, to silence.

Q. When you say, 'In daily life *today'*, are you implying that language has changed?
A. The use of sounds is only a fraction of our communication. Today, most people rely heavily on the verbal.

The art of true communication lies in tranquillity and its delightful variety of spontaneous expressions. In many ancient languages the sound was closer to that to which it referred. Words had much more dynamic power. Today, at least in our Western languages, words have lost their proximity with the real. As we have become more taken by achievement and attainment, so our centres have become ever more ejected into that world of end-gaining. Our language, being a brain activity, has followed our desires accordingly. You can see around you more and more objects to be acquired, and each object calls for a new sound to distinguish it from other objects. This is far indeed from those sounds which come out of, express and point to, our essential nature.

Q. Even when living in freedom from the subject-object relationship, are we not finally bound to time?
A. Man is always creating time. This psychological time is essentially the past and we continually revive the past through it. It is thought based on memory. In fact what we call the future is only a modified past. Psychological time is never in the now but, like a pendulum, is in constant movement from past to future, from future to present, in rapid succession. It exists only on the horizontal plane, the plane of having/becoming, pleasure/displeasure, grasping/avoidance, security/insecurity. It is the source of misery and conflict and alienates us from pure existence. Understanding psychological time and space is the way to meditation and right functioning. Chronological, astronomical time is equally based on memory, but it is a memory functioning freely without the intervention of an ego, of will. Events proceed in orderly succession, and since there is no movement between a so-called past and future, there is no conflict.

It is the interference of a self-image which separates

observer from observed. In true observation, observer and observed are one. This is the beginning of complete understanding. When we think, we think either in terms of the past or the future, but life is always now. To live in the now implies a mind free from end-gaining and recapitulation. In presence is contained eternity, all possible happening. Everything is a present thought and thought and object are one. Time is thought and thought appears in time. Beauty and joy are only revealed in the now.

Q. Why would we create time?
A. For the delectation of the I-image. But when you live in your real nature it is delectable from moment to moment! Fundamentally there is no time because the moment is one with consciousness.

Q. Does space exist?
A. Space is a concept. We cannot think of space without reference to tangible bodies which we see as other than or outside our own body. Several perceptions are required for an idea of extension.

Q. You are talking about space as a concept. Can it not be experienced as perception?
A. You can come to a feeling of spaciousness when you go beyond the physical structure of the body and encounter the subtle or energy body. But there is still a vague centre of reference.

Q. You said that time is memory. What is memory?
A. Memory which functions without the limitations of the self-image is completely integrated in cosmic memory, the all-possibility, whose archetypes are in us as the tree is in the seed. Functional memory appears spontane-

ously when needed in different situations. Spontaneous thinking is grounded in functional memory. However, we rarely give memory this freedom of function. Psychological memory recalls constantly. It is a fortress for the survival of the 'me', the idea of being an individual. The categories of past, present and future are mere conventions for the survival of this image.

Q. When I meet someone a second time, for example, is it possible to use only functional memory?
A. Absolutely! Functional memory may recall the name, face and previous circumstances, but take note that you quickly form opinions about people and that this psychological memory colours your second meeting with the flavour of the first. You bring preconceived ideas with you. With this kind of memory there can be no real meeting. You do not let the other come to you in newness and you in turn take the old with you. There is no love, no affection.

Q. It seems clear that the almost continual feeling or assertion of the 'me' is a protection against a fear of being in forgetfulness, Lethe. It is the fear of dying. If I let go of psychological memory can I be sure that functional memory will go on and I will be able to continue to live in the world?
A. Our senses, organs, brains, personality traits, the whole body, when left to themselves are tools which function efficiently and easily. Most of the time, however, they are impeded from organic functioning by a process of reaction and compensation, like and dislike, analysis, categorising and judging. Become accustomed to dying, to moments when this process is absent. In the absence of psychological memory your living in the world is new at every moment.

In all doing and thinking the 'I' should take a step back so that motiveless alertness and the whole body organ can come into play. Practically speaking this is the first step. The tools of existence are not problematic. It is only when you identify with what are simply tools that problems arise. When you let functions remain impersonal functions, they become infinitely more efficient and varied. In simple function is beauty. Remember that love and freedom have nothing to do with memory, but when you think of love and freedom you make them ideas using memory. Stay with the living understanding before the reflex to objectify and appropriate comes in.

THE ART OF LISTENING

Free from selection

Q. You say that when the body-mind is freed of psychological interference it comes spontaneously to listening which is the tool of self-inquiry. Would you talk more about this?

A. The discovery of your real nature cannot come about through memory. It comes through multidimensional attention, which occurs naturally when memory is absent. This innate attention is listening. When you are in listening you feel yourself in vastness, in immensity, where there is no listener or looker. Only in listening can the transmutation from having knowledge to knowing as being happen. Listening is an art with which you must become acquainted. It is being open to all the expressions of life. Life's expressions are never repetitious. There may be analogy but there's no repetition. See that apparent repetition is only memory. Listening is a welcoming of life without reference to the already known. Real discovery is only in the immediate moment itself. We can never comprehend the unknown through the known. We are educated to experience, to look with motive, to interpret, but we must explore the possibility of living as non-experience. This exploration takes place in non-reactional listening. In unconditioned listening we are open to all possibilities, and in the absence of restriction direct perception occurs.

Q. How can I become acquainted with the art of listening?

A. Only by living it, as a musician learns to listen by listening. There are no techniques, disciplines or ideas that you can substitute for listening itself. All these are sweets for the ego. The more you become acquainted with listening through listening, the freer you are of the self-image. The teaching is only to bring you back to listening. In listening there's no listening to; you find yourself in openness, in the listening non-state itself.

Q. You say listening comes through listening. Could you be more explicit about what it actually is?

A. Listening is not a cerebral process. It is not a function. It is an open sensitivity free from anticipation, achievement or attainment. It is not an attitude one assumes nor is it confined to the ears, just as when you understand something and you say 'I see' it has nothing to do with the organs of sight.

Q. How can I come to this global sensitivity?

A. If you let your attention go to your ear, you'll feel that it is constantly grasping. It is the same with the eye, the mind and all your organs. Let the grasping go and you will find your whole body is spontaneously an organ of sensitivity. The ear is merely a channel for this global sensation. It is not an end in itself. What is heard is also felt, seen, smelled, touched. Your five senses, intelligence and imagination are freed and come into play. You feel it as being completely expanded in space, without centre or border. The ego which is a contraction can find no hold in this presence and anxiety, like or dislike dissolve. You feel this wholeness without feeling it. You feel it but you cannot categorise it into any known feeling.

The sense organs are only pointers to global awareness. But generally they appropriate the apparent object and prevent it from unfolding in your completeness. Try to hear and look without focusing on specific things. Let your hearing and seeing find their organic multi-dimensionality. When there is no goal or motive in your hearing, it becomes unconditioned listening. All that comes up is in this listening but there is no listener to focus on any sound. In the end all sounds vanish in hearing itself. Then you are one with the moment. There is no space and thus no time. Real listening is spaceless and timeless. Since it is listening as being and not a function it does not depend on an object heard. Listening without representation is like a magnet to which all objects point and in which they vanish. Listening refers to itself. It is the natural state. So you come to the deep conclusion that all sound points to silence, that silence is before and after hearing.

Q. Is it not natural to want to listen to and look at what is pleasant and beautiful? Isn't some choice inevitable in the world today? You have often said that we must make a choice in life to see the most beautiful things in our society. Who is to say what is beautiful?
A. We are composed in harmony and where it is reflected will be attractive to us. But this harmony has nothing to do with what is commonly called pleasant or beautiful. When we live in beauty there is a spontaneous discrimination which is not based on the conventional. See when something appeals to you because it is in accord with the prevailing taste and when it appeals to your whole being, which is timeless.

Q. Why are the senses grasping?
A. The mind controls the body in fractions. This is a deep conditioning that we take for granted. The brain func-

tions successively. For global sensation to function, the everyday brain activity must go into abeyance. In your natural state this happens very often, but you live in an unnatural way where there is constant agitation, mind activity. Thus you have lost the global body feeling.

Listening is passive and active. Passive because there is no interference of a controlling ego, no memory, and thus it is completely receptive. Active in that it is alert at every moment. Listening is awareness. It does not require endless practice which involves fighting habits. Simply be aware that you do not listen. Spend one morning not concluding or interpreting. Let your ego rest only for one morning and observe.

Q. When you say your whole body comes into play, where is the mind?
A. Generally the mental function dominates our senses, our perception. For global listening, which is your organic state, to occur, this domination must stop. In stillness the mind functions, taking its place with the rest of the body functions, but its functioning no longer refers to a centre. It merely perceives and names. A mind which is simply in movement is not a problem. On the contrary when the intellect is grounded in silence everything is spontaneously referred to this ground.

You see a rose. The intellect perceives and names it. Perfect functioning. But then it goes on and begins to interfere with the perception preventing it from unfolding in direct perception. The imaginary person, the centre of viewpoints, sees the colour and compares it, or likes it, dislikes it perhaps. It thinks about its beauty or remembers some past reference. But during this activity where is the real perfume of the rose?

Psychological activity is fractional and successive. There can only be one percept or concept at a time, so it is impossible to feel the wholeness of the rose with the everyday functioning of the mind. You can only add up its parts. But the true perfume of the rose, what it really is, is not in a collection of fractions. When you step back from stressing the parts, when the mind becomes still, the rose comes to you, unfolds in you in all her glory. The perfume invades you completely. The rose is you. You are one.

So in listening let the mind be still as your legs are still when you don't need them. Let the words, sensations, situations blossom in you and deliver their perfume. Live with this perfume.

Q. I sometimes feel resistance to what you say. I am sceptical and cannot believe you.
A. Firstly, don't worry about believing! I am not interested in belief. It is the mind which believes and you are not the mind. So leave belief and disbelief behind. Look at your resistance. Don't analyse its whys and wherefores. Simply take note that you don't listen, that you react. Very often when people think they have understood, it is a kind of reaction based on interpretation or sympathy or aversion. Listening is welcoming without interpretation. Take note that you are afraid to give up interpreting because it means the ego can no longer produce. Welcoming has nothing to do with agreeing. It has its own taste!

Be alert and observe both the words you hear and your psychosomatic field. Watch every movement towards qualifying, judging, analysing. When you see that your listening is not free from interference, that everything is referred to a subject, a point of view, then the cycle of reaction loses its dynamism. When it is put under close observation, the psychological process is arrested. It is a thief who can only work in secret. As soon as the light is turned on him, his activity is exposed and he becomes powerless. When the agitated mind relaxes, you may find yourself in a timeless moment of real listening.

Q. It is very difficult for me not to try to remember what you say. I don't want to forget it!

A. Never try to retain what is said here. If you do, you buy your Christmas present with your own money when the gift that comes to you as an offering will give much more joy! Let the words lose their concreteness. When you emphasise the language, the meaning, the words lose their flavour. The moment you listen without retaining, what is said sooner or later strikes your whole being and there comes a sudden ripening. So live with the perfume of these sayings and do not try to grasp their meaning. There comes a moment when the essence of what is said comes up and you are taken by understanding as being. It is completely non-mental. You cannot come to it. It is offered.

Q. What do you mean, 'offered'?

A. It is a way of speaking. There is no one who offers and no one who receives. It comes from nowhere else but arises in you as you. In using the expression 'offered', I want to emphasise that there is nothing you can do to attain being understanding. You must listen in the same relaxed and receptive way that you might read a poem or look at a painting. Feel the rhythm, sound and colour, and do not conclude.

Q. How can there be solutions to the questions of life if we live without conclusions?

A. I am not saying that there are no conclusions, but the solution comes directly from the situation itself and not from your projection. Each situation is unique and has its own answer. When you listen to a situation from your wholeness without the interference of an I-image, there is direct perception. Then the situation concludes in you. If you try to manipulate a solution, you may arrange things temporarily to suit your ego but you remain on the personal and conflictual level.

The mind can change all the furniture around in the room but the walls remain. Why live within walls? Your being, peace and ultimate satisfaction lie in the limitless and timeless.

DISCERNMENT

Knowing beyond knowledge

The natural involuntary reflex of our brain is attention, just as the inbuilt reflex of the eye is seeing, the ear hearing, the skin tactile feeling, and so on. Since it is a natural reflex no named object is needed for seeing, hearing, attention. When we are attracted to an object there is perception, the cognition of form. Perception belongs to the sense organs. When you walk through a forest you perceive trees, colours and sounds without naming them as 'tree', 'blue', 'birdsong'. The name appears and disappears without your being aware of it, so it can hardly be called a name. It is more a vague reference to memory. This belongs to the organic function of the brain, to cognition. When the need to differentiate arises, the reference remains and becomes concretised as a concept, a name. This is recognition based on functional memory. It is a process completely inherent to our human nature and still belongs to the motiveless attention of the brain. The movement from percept to concept or form to name takes place spontaneously in a fraction of a second and does not refer to an agent.

Very often, however, the percept and concept are referred to an agent, a supposed centre. This 'controller' is the habitual idea, strengthened over millions of years, of a separate entity. Each so-called individual centre develops its own patterns of analysis, interpretation, justification, comparison, judgement, and so on, and imposes these on the percept and its concept. This psychological involvement hinders the perception, that is, the senses, preventing them from being able to fully unfold. What remains is an alienation of the pure concept into a representation based on psychological memory. The name then loses its transparency and refers to a collection, a crystallisation, of reactions. When naming is weighed down by points of view it loses its true symbolic value as a window from silence to silence. Mistaking psychological representation for perception is a symptom of illusion and maintains the attitude of separate observer and observed.

Q. You said that when the need to differentiate arises there is concept. From where does this need arise?
A. To function as a human being with others in the world one must know the difference between a shoe and a hat. The concretisation of cognition into concept gives rise to language. Language is an agreement, a convention. It is a functional orientation within global awareness, and when it remains purely functional it is automatically economical, appropriate, and arises and dies in awareness. From the point of view of the individual, however, the need to think is only to maintain the person. The idea of being 'a person' is, like all ideas, localised in the brain, It is a contraction away from global sensitivity. It is such an overriding idea that it brings all thought and sensation under its dominion. Thus, concept dominates percept, the head the body, the verbal language has taken priority over other more important forms of communication.

The distinction between the psychological which refers to an 'I' and the purely functional which is not centralised must be clearly seen.

Q. You have said that 'naming is a window from silence to silence'. What do you mean by this?
A. The name exists merely to bring the object to our attention. But since a percept and concept cannot exist together, the name must immediately disappear, leaving the percept to dissolve in attention without thought. An object has no autonomous existence. It lives only in consciousness.

Q. Is this unclouded attention the silence you speak of?
A. Attention is still localised as brain function. Silence is the background of all function. The relaxed brain is not at a standstill but is in continual gentle movement. It is a pulsation that does not come to concretisation. These movements arise and die in your complete emptiness of projection, your fullness of silence. Attention is an expression of this stillness which is your natural being.

Q. When the concept brings the percept to our attention what happens?
A. When the concept has disappeared the percept loses its localisation in one sense and all the senses are given freedom to unfold. In this welcoming the object loses its objectivity, revealing only the welcoming itself. This I sometimes call a pure or direct perception. There is nothing known outside the senses. There is apparent stimulation but the stimulating 'object' is known only through the senses. It is the unfolding of the senses that reveals their home ground. The undressed known reveals the unknown.

Q. Would you talk more about the actual process of the unfolding of the senses?
A. The percept is apprehended by a sense organ and brought to attention by the concept. When the concept

does not grasp the object, that is, when it does not become a representation, it is automatically transposed to all the senses. In this letting go of objectification the senses unfold in relaxed attention and there is a moment when the emphasis shifts from the senses to the attention. This attention is still perceptible as a localisation in the brain and when this localisation is seen you are taken by a feeling of expansion. This is global awareness which is at the threshold of being, your natural non-state.

The unfolding of the senses therefore ultimately takes you to your stillness where there is no object and thus no tension and conflict. You feel how all functioning comes and goes in this stillness free from agitation. Like a sound it appears in silence and disappears in silence.

Q. Is this what is meant by 'every object points to consciousness'?
A. An object is name and form. Name and form belong to the body, senses and mind. An object exists only because there's a subject. But on closer examination this so-called subject, with which we have identified, is also seen to be an object. It can be perceived by a higher subject sometimes called 'the witness' for pedagogical reasons. The witness does not exist. There is only witnessing, which is awareness, consciousness, our natural state.

When there is identification with the relative subject, dualism is maintained and the object cannot empty itself of objectivity. But when the subject is seen as a function of mind, as having no autonomy, no substance, name and form are given up. In this letting go the object loses objectivity and refers immediately to our totality, consciousness without object.

Q. When there is identification with a subject one is locked into concepts. Is not the regression ad infinitum

of subjects that belongs to philosophical Idealism only this?
A. Consciousness is knowing as being. It is totality. From the point of view of the mind every object asks for a subject, a subject asks for an object. This so-called subject is an object, too, perceived by consciousness. In this is eternal joy, love and freedom.

One must make the distinction between what is and what exists. Existence lives in consciousness. Consciousness expresses itself in existence. It is the totality and is in no way diminished or augmented by existence.

Q. What are the steps to come to non-subjective observation free from the person?
A. When an object comes before consciousness and you don't relate yourself, the ego, to the object, then there is no intention or expectation. The mind is not busy waiting for a result. Observation then is of non-reactional attention. You do not do anything to the object or try to derive something from it. In this non-relationship the mind goes into abeyance simply because it no longer has a role to play. Effortlessly, you find yourself simply open, free from the past.

When you are waiting for an experience all the past is still active. You are still affectively bound to the object, wanting a conclusion, wanting to modify, analyse or transform the present. In this way you hope to give yourself an experience. See what it means to just be there, to be present without any centre to your psyche, subconscious or unconscious. There is simply watching. In this watching you are not tethered to the past. You are free and the distinction between observer and observed – I and myself – withers away. You are left in complete stillness. A new sensitivity is born when the cerebral motion comes to an end. Thought, emotivity, intention die away and you find yourself in the original quietness of body, senses and mind. There is no longer any movement from a centre, a person, but movement which simultaneously takes place throughout your whole being.

Q. Can pure perception without the interference of the I-image be cultivated?
A. Absolutely. You can be knowingly in a landscape without remaining in the frame of form and name. When a painter is not fixed in the form and name he paints more than a tree or a roof. He paints what is not visible in the form and name. A tree that is not referred to oneself has infinite possibilities. One must not frame an object with memory and anticipation. When there is simply looking without mental intervention there is openness, welcoming, and the object relaxes and blossoms in the hospitality of one's whole being. The idea of the person, continuous thinking, is a defence against this welcoming, this openness where there is nothing to protect or affirm. In openness the object is weaker than the subject and there is a transfer of energy to the receiving position. This is a direct perception.

Q. What is the difference between the perception of a very young infant and a sage? Do they not both perceive directly without the interference of an ego?
A. Yes. Both are equally free from psychological interference. In this the wise become like little children. But the child does not know the object in himself as the sage does. In an infant, perception is instinctive and not conscious and there may be identification with the object. In the one who knows his being, the faculty of perceiving is spontaneously orientated to this knowing. All functioning refers to it.

Q. Is pure perception localised anywhere? In other words is there still duality in conscious perception?
A. The percept is still a brain function because it appears through the senses but when it is not fixed in the cerebral it is drawn to global awareness as eagerly as a moth is drawn to the light. Global awareness is still, however, an awareness 'of', an emphasis on the subject, a feeling of wholeness. It is perceptible to itself, a subtle duality. It is not knowing oneself in *sahaja* where there is no emphasis on the subject which is the source of all functions and states and is unaffected by the presence or absence of objects.

Q. Will you speak more about the shift in emphasis from perception to attention, from the objective to the subjective aspect?
A. At first the object of perception is in the foreground, and attention, or the subject-aspect, is in the background. When attention is noticed and sustained through relaxation and the absence of psychological intervention, interpretation, judgement, analysis, and so on, it expands and at a certain point there is a kind of implosion, where the object-aspect shifts to the background and attention is in the foreground. Now the subject-aspect is emphasised. The switch-over in emphasis is the sudden release of localisation in the brain to global 'feeling' beyond the senses. This expansion is the immediate prelude to the dissolving of attention as a percept, the expanded 'I', into pure awareness, where there is no longer emphasis on a subject or object and where there are no qualifications. It is often misleadingly called the ultimate subject.

Q. If I understand correctly a so-called object reveals itself as the contents of body and mind and when these contents are in turn seen as objects of perception one is

left simply in awareness without the brain activity of
motive and goal. This is an emptiness of all objectification. My question is: How can emptiness be fullness?
One may know an absence of objects but surely this is
not the fullness of being you speak of.
A. This is a very interesting question. When the last activity of protecting an I-image has gone into abeyance one is
left simply with being there. It is a directionless presence
without brain activity, as you said. In this directionless
silence where am I? The first impact may be one of feeling lost because one cognises an absence of activity; this
is the negative part, sometimes called the 'blank state'.
At this crucial moment you must remember you are not a
state and become acquainted with non-directional emptiness. Find yourself in the creativity of silence exploring the non-cerebral field, the directionless. Then there
comes a point where there is nothing left to observe and
the – by now – very subtle division between observer
and observed spontaneously vanishes. This is 'being
meditation' where no one is aware of anything. No one
moves in daily life. There is no restriction on individuality. There is only wholeness, entirety. It is a non-state.
Then when action is called for, action appears; when
speech is necessary, sound appears; movement occurs
when movement is necessary. You use your faculties or
sense organs when required. Everything, every percept,
concept, feeling, emotion, comes out of the totality of
your beingness.

Q. Where objects are no longer objects but are expressions of one's totality, then the apparent independence of
the world must be an illusion.
A. The so-called objective world that we take for granted
is created every moment you objectify it in thinking. Its
apparent autonomy is only a projection. To say that the

world was created at a certain point is merely second-hand information, what we call common sense. The real creation is a prolongation, an expression in space and time of the stillness which you are. It is in constant actualisation.

Q. Why is it that men like Immanuel Kant or Einstein could not come to fully understand the nature of existence?

A. Kant recognised that the world was known through the body-mind but he still identified with this body-mind and projected a thing-in-itself 'outside'. Einstein did not come to know the nature of existence because he identified with it. We can never come to the unknown by pursuing the known. We can only come to know all that fundamentally we are not. We can never, with the mind, know the whole, we can only know parts. Our original mistake is to identify with our psychosomatic structure and not recognise that it is also a perception. When identification with the body ceases there is no outside or inside, and the world, including the body and all its senses, is reabsorbed in globality which is sometimes called the ultimate perceiver. What is unknowable in terms of perception is then living knowing. The apparent independence of the world is based only on the false idea that identifies consciousness with the body. When the body is also seen as an object of consciousness, how can there be an autonomous world outside it? Infinity is not simply a geometrical representation. The infinity of being is all-encompassing.

Q. You said that pure attention is on the threshold of awareness. What then is the difference between attention and awareness?

A. Attention is still brain function though free from psychological interference. As attention broadens, brain function slows down and attention flows into awareness. Completely limitless attention and awareness are one and the same.

Q. Is this awareness our real nature?
A. In awareness there is no limitation of brain function but there is still a conceptual duality: 'I am aware of something.' This something is global functioning, energy uncontaminated by the cerebral structure and the senses. Here you find yourself at the threshold of your timeless being. You are in the nearness of your real nature where nobody is aware of anything. It is the background of all function.

Q. How does one go from the threshold to the stillness beyond all movement?
A. You cannot cross the threshold by any activity. Only abide there and you are spontaneously taken.

Q. What is the nature of this abiding?
A. It is 'waiting without waiting', to use Heidegger's phrase, a state of openness without goal or motive. It is akin to wonder, to admiration without an object. In living unconditional openness you are taken by your essential being. But you must wait to be taken. There is no going.

Q. At the threshold itself is there still subject-object relationship, duality?
A. At the threshold of being, openness is still a perception. It is the perfume of inevitable self-knowing. Abiding in this inevitability brings tremendous relaxation and letting-go of all residues of individuality. In this freedom from the past one's totality unfolds and there comes a sudden moment when it attracts to itself the

remaining residues of the person. These residues have by now lost their concreteness and exist in this instant merely as representations which are then absorbed for ever in the magnetic light of pure being. Individuality, the sense of authorship, psychological memory vanish, never to return, and you are established in the stillness of presence without the idea of becoming. After awakening there is nothing to gain or lose.

Q. Is there no feeling after such a momentous event?
A. On the phenomenal level there is a feeling close to thankfulness. Thankfulness for its own sake, for there is no one left to give and receive thanks. It is offering. It is pure love.

THE PROGRESSIVE AND THE DIRECT APPROACH

Enlightenment is not an experience

In the spiritual adventure one proceeds by either the progressive way or the direct way. A way takes you from one point to another. This is the logical procedure when you want to obtain something. But you cannot attain what you already are.

In the progressive way you go from relative existence to the ultimate principle we can call being. It is a path of purification and elimination and is recognised in stages, that is, through experiences. In all experiences, you remain in the subject-object relationship. This subject-object relationship is an expression of life but it is not life itself.

Q. Why do you say that the path of stages or different levels keeps you in the subject-object relationship?
A. Progression can only be known through experience, comparison and interpretation, in other words, through memory. There must be a centre of reference, otherwise, how could you talk of stages?

All levels belong to the mind. But what you already and constantly are is not a level, nor a state, nor an experience. These are impermanent and have a beginning and an end, but your real nature is causeless and timeless. How then can you reach the non-state through a series of states? These states may bring you delightful experiences, it is true, but they are sugar for the I-image, nothing else. Stages are a creation of the ego to keep it alive in a more and more subtle way. Although they bring about a certain purification and elimination, they can never bring you a hair's breadth nearer to the non-state.

Q. What is a non-state? I know only states.
A. Any time when the I-image is absent such as in moments of astonishment, wonder, love, admiration, where there is no time and space, there is the non-state. In it there is always the element of surprise. It cannot be predicted or attained. Admiration or wonder is the background of all perception. It is love, the origin of all giving.

Q. Is there no object of admiration such as the feeling of oneness, for example?
A. When you admire something you are in a relationship of separation. You remain in quantity and comparison. In real admiring you are one with the perception. There is no one to admire and nothing to be admired. All is expanded, light, with no centre and no periphery. You are nowhere. Admiring basks in its own warmth.

There is no reference to the already known. It is an unexpected gesture free from motive and result. In admiring there is no acquisition, only liberation. It is the taste of yourself.

Q. Does not elimination of past conditioning occur in the progressive way?
A. When you proceed from the relative to the ultimate in stages your ego remains engaged. There is end-gaining.

You are bound to the object. You may undo earlier conditioning but you merely learn a new conditioning, often one that is less flexible and interesting! When even the slightest emphasis is put on attaining, you continue the habit of objectifying your freedom and joy. You still say, 'I have experienced this.' You are still someone doing something. You remain in fraction. You take yourself for a prisoner with the goal of freedom. But the premise itself is an illusion. There is nothing to attain, nothing to lose.

Q. So is bondage an imagined state, or is there any reality to it?
A. The constant attempt to find ourselves in the perception is very deeply rooted in us. But what we fundamentally are can never be an object of perception. Don't try to free yourself from the body. The idea of becoming free from the body belongs to the body. Accept the perception of your body. Really accept it functionally, its sensation, feelings, reactions, tensions. Don't be content with ideas, with hearsay. As you look deeper you will see that it is nothing other than the five senses. When the senses are freed from the controlling ego, you will come to a body that is completely homogeneous. The mind is a cage but when you really look, you can see no prisoner.

Q. What is the outcome of the progressive approach if one remains bound in the subject-object relationship?
A. The result of all progressive ways is what we call the 'blank state'. When you proceed through levels and experiences you never come out of the pattern of trying to objectify your real nature. You may find many interesting objects, different energy centres, all kinds of ecstatic and dramatic feelings. There may come about a certain purification but you are inevitably brought to a tragic

moment. The final stage can only be the absence of all known objects. It is complete elimination, but because of the habit of objectifying you make of the absence a state, a blank state. You are still bound to a subtle subject-object relationship and it is very difficult for this last object to be reabsorbed into the non-state.

Q. Do you mean that we need not be empty of objects to come to the stillness that is behind all phenomena?
A. The blank state is still a state you enter and leave. When you have voluntarily reduced all known objects to one last object, emptiness, you are in a tremendous enigma: there is presence in the absence of objects, but this presence does not remain in the presence of objects.

Q. Why do you call the blank state tragic?
A. In the presence of absence you live in a desert because you have used will to renounce objects. In a certain way you are fixed in the absence of objects. This absence is a state without flavour. It may be St. John of the Cross's 'Dark Night of the Soul'. It is a most tragic thing to feel abandoned in emptiness without knowing the fullness, the silence, which is not affected by the absence or presence of phenomena. In real giving up there's no will. The object gives itself up through understanding.

Q. You have said that existence is the film and we are the light that makes the film possible. What would you call the blank state in this analogy?
A. The blank state is the empty screen. When you have, through will, emptied the screen of all its pictures you are fixed on the emptiness. Because you have been concentrating on the screen it is difficult in this moment to realise that what you are has nothing to do with the screen.

You now face the emptiness and cannot feel behind you the light, the fullness you have systematically ignored. The progressive paths start with the screen and its pictures, the accepted notion of dual existence, subject and object. Through a process of observation, elimination, unveiling or exploring the object, one struggles to come to wholeness. But practically, once you have adopted the duality as your starting-point, that is, the attitude of being bound to the perception, it is unlikely that you will be able to come out of it. Practice only reinforces it. In the direct way you go immediately to the wholeness and every perception is seen only in the light of wholeness. Even if this is not yet a reality for you, you still proceed as if it were. This is very important.

Q. So there is nothing at all we can learn from experiences?
A. You will learn much more by asking yourself what exactly is an experience. Do we ever really experience a situation or do we experience only our reactions to it? Generally our initial reaction is not even felt. All too often the mind avoids its own reactions by escaping in many devious ways. This double reaction is what we generally assume to be life or experience.

Q. Can you give me an example of double reaction?
A. You have had a bad day at work and when you come home you shout at the children who are playing loudly as usual. Your mood is merely looking for an outlet. Reactions happen almost constantly on a more subtle level. You might meet someone and be reminded of someone else so that you don't really see the person you are with. Or you might be bored and not know it because you avoid facing the lack by filling your time with activities. In order to fully experience anything the mind must be

empty, free from memory emotivity, gain and expectation. What we call experience is generally the repetition of sensation or the projections of memory. Mechanical repetition brings boredom and many people, rather than face the roots of the boredom, look for supposedly deep 'spiritual' states. In this sense the mystical quest masquerades as the spiritual quest. In the end the mind adores its own fabrications. It is hungry for satisfaction but satisfaction and pleasure are only unabsorbed sensation.

In the field of technology a certain amount of accumulation is necessary but this does not create a problem. However, on the psychological plane, the accumulation of what we call experiences merely strengthens the ego. For a real happening to occur our likes and dislikes, points of view, our attachment to the pleasure—pain structure, must come to an end. The word 'experience' as we use it in our language has a beginning and an end. It is discontinuous, a state we enter and leave. It belongs to an experiencer. A true experience then is really a non-experience since there is no experiencing agent. It is grounded in wholeness, not in time and space. It leaves no residue as memory, is not comparable and cannot be sought. A non-experience appears spontaneously in the first opening. It is the background of all states. You know this non-experience from moments in life when everything has been done and there's no projection for the next thing, when your mind is completely unfurnished. Generally you take the absence of furniture as the absence of something. You objectify the absence, you remain in relation to it. Don't emphasise the absence. Come to the absence of the absence.

Q. What is *samadhi*? Does it belong to the progressive or direct way?
A. *Samadhi* is the attuning to a representation that stimu-

lates in you a very profound emotion, for example, full-ness, peace, joy, God, love, the Divine Mother. In the end the representation becomes very transparent and fleeting. But *samadhi* is still a state you enter and leave. There is still a subject who is aware of the subtlest forms. *Samadhi* belongs mainly to the progressive way. In the direct way it may occur accidentally but it is given no significance because it has nothing to do with the non-state, *sahaja*. Do you know the story of the great yogi who asked his disciple for a glass of water and while the disciple was fetching it the yogi fell into deep *samadhi*? He remained so for thirty years and was soon surrounded by admirers. When he emerged he asked for the glass of water!

Q. Is *kundalini* an experience, too, like *samadhi*?
A. *Kundalini* belongs to a technique. There is still the belief that there is something to attain, something to find. You may go to the end of the purification of the body but you are still left with the purified empty body. As we said, when you are accustomed to the progressive approach it is very difficult for this last object to vanish in the observer. All practice belongs to the mind. In practice your intellect loses its sensitivity and flexibility because it is put into a frame.

Q. Without some kind of discipline I feel I will not change at all!
A. Who will not change? What will not change? Begin by questioning your desire to change. Your practices are only an escape from facing the first question. Through discipline you may alter the position of all the objects on your table but that is superficial and all the objects slide off! See that you are constantly escaping from facing your ego head on. The mind is sly and seduces you down many roads rather than release its control on you. When

you see something clearly the pattern loses its power. No amount of striving can bring you to clear seeing. When you see your mechanism clearly the energy, the axis, of your being immediately shifts and transformation occurs.

Q. Is this immediate facing the 'direct way'?
A. As we said, in the direct way, which strictly speaking is not a way, you face the ultimate principle immediately. You accept as a possibility what you have heard, that you are not body, senses and mind, but the light behind all perceptions. The basic supposition of the direct way is that your global non-state is already there, is natural to you, and it 'waits' for the deep relaxation of the habits of mind and body. This is God, grace, the presence that appears in the openings between your egotistical pursuits. It is always present. Any movement to attain it is thus a going away because when you want something you suppose you lack it. No amount of effort can persuade Presence to appear. There is no spiritual evolution. Your natural being is not in the becoming process. When you are convinced of this it brings a new dimension to living, an opening that is beyond all becoming. In the direct way you live with this dimension from the beginning. Then there is never an emphasis on the object, the perception. All objects appear and disappear in the background and serve only to reveal the background. You can never obtain what you are. It reveals itself by itself.

Q. You talk about observation, being the knower, which might be interpreted as a kind of introversion; on the other hand, you say, let the sensation come up, surrender to the perception. How can one resolve this?
A. The terms 'introversion' and 'extroversion' have been created by modern psychology. Some even say that all

that is perceived belongs to extroversion and the ultimate perceiver refers to introversion. But when you look at the ultimate perceiver you cannot speak of in or out since it belongs neither in space nor time. So we can't use these terms introversion and extroversion in our way of thinking.

In the Yoga Sutra of Patanjali the word *pratiahara* is often translated as 'withdrawal of the senses'. But don't see this withdrawal as an ingoing, a contraction, of the senses. Rather, withdrawal means a withdrawal of emphasis on the senses. In this letting go there is expansion without any more concentration. When the emphasis is no longer fixed on the object, the senses, but is in multi-dimensional attention itself, there comes a moment when they unfold completely and suddenly are absorbed in non-dimensional awareness. Here, there is no goal or result to be obtained, no satisfaction or pleasure, for this awareness is itself what you are seeking.

In letting go, tremendous energy is released, energy that was fixed through habit. It then reorchestrates and finds its balance in your wholeness. There is integration and the senses automatically come to their right place in the symphony of life. All that is perceived lives in you but you don't live in it. There is nothing 'outside'. All the mystery of human beings is in you. The world is in you. There is no progression. We only must know how to look. The problem is not in the world but in our way of looking.

Q. How important is intellectual understanding in the direct way?
A. Understanding is indispensable in the direct way. It is the work of the intellect to recognise its limits and remind you that what you are is not a concept or an experience. The scientist emphasises the object world.

There is the reflex to express his knowledge immediately, to say 'I understand.' But the truth-seeker lives in the global intuition which precedes the 'I understand.' He knows it cannot be objectified. The intellect is grounded in global consciousness and in its transparency all perceptions are referred to consciousness so that in the moment when consciousness is empty of all objects, this emptiness too is referred to consciousness. It is not made an object but is reabsorbed in the background, *sahaja*, the light of activity and non-activity. Thus in the direct way the blank state is never actualised. The movement from emptiness to fullness is the moment of grace.

Q. There is still elimination of the ego in the direct path, so is it not in a sense progressive too?
A. We live in time and space. Although the axis shifts in one moment it takes time for past habits to fall away. Accidentally, therefore, we use elements of progression for clarification, for example, the feeling body-work we do. The emphasis, however, is never on the object but on the ultimate non-state. The perception is faced in openness and in this openness the object is exalted and tells us its secret. The object is a mirror, a pointer, in the same way that we know the moon is in the sky when we see it reflected in the water. The pointing of the object is a kind of jubilation in the direct way. It is through the object that the ultimate subject is revealed. The presence of objects finds its real significance in the presence that is your real being.

In the progressive way you evaluate each fraction to a known position. In the direct way you establish a non-relationship with the object. Then it belongs to your completeness.

Q. What do you understand by the Zen saying 'First there are mountains, then there are no mountains, then there are mountains again'?
A. First you are aware only of objects. You are identified with the mountains. Then you become aware that objects exist because they are perceived, because you are. Attention is then on the perceiver, not the objects. But quickly the intellect reminds you that the perceiver that can be perceived is also an object and you are taken by the ultimate perceiver, awareness itself, the 'no mountains'. This is direct perception. But as long as the body exists in space and time, the senses function spontaneously in the world. Without the restrictions imposed on them by a perceiver, sense perceptions unfold and there are mountains again. These are no longer perceived as objects but as facets of one harmonious Reality. They are no longer an objectification in space but an extension of silence, expressions of the totality you are. It is a completely different distribution of energy in yourself.

Q. How does the direct way deal with the mechanical reflex of the brain towards succession and progression?
A. Glimpses of reality appear and when the emphasis is on the background, the source of the glimpses, and not on concretising them into a stage, the mechanical reflexes to interpret dissolve through lack of use.

In the progressive way you constantly refer to experience through comparison with your previous state. You remain in your own darkness. The emphasis is on *avidya*, ignorance. In the direct way you don't emphasise ignorance but look to the light, to *vidya*. It is a question of where you put the accent.

Q. Does meditation differ in the two ways?
A. Absolutely. In the progressive approach meditation is

a discipline to still the mind and bring it to an absence of thought. But the mind can never be permanently still. To associate no-thought with silence is false identification. Silence is beyond the presence and absence of thought.

You can never try to be still. You can never try to meditate. When you see what appears to be not still in you, your seeing is itself from stillness. Only from quietness can you feel agitation, nervousness, and so on. If you were in the agitation, how could you know it? When you are in a train travelling at 150 mph, you have no feeling of the speed. But when you stand on the ground outside you see it streak by.

In the direct way sitting meditation is used only as a laboratory to watch how your mechanism functions. You give no hold to what you watch so that from the beginning the emphasis is on listening and watching. At other times the word 'meditation' refers to your background, the stillness or presence in which all appears spontaneously.

I read an old Jewish story that tells the difference between meditation as a discipline to still the mind and living meditation as the background of action and non-action. Once, there lived a father and a son who were both great sages, but the father was the greater. One day he was passing a house and heard a baby crying. He went inside and saw his son immersed in meditation while his child was crying in the cradle. The father said to his son, 'My son, I didn't know you had such a small mind. In meditation I can still hear a fly moving about.'

MEDITATION

Where there is no meditator there is nothing to meditate upon

Meditation is not a mental or physical activity. We cannot say what meditation is in the field of objective knowledge. It is not anything perceivable. It is not in the field of existence, energy and motion, but is a non-state beyond all states. Meditation is the source of motion and motionlessness. So, clearly, it is not a function, not something you can do.

Being in meditation brings a new way of living from moment to moment, a living that cannot be divided into compartments: some time for business, some for eating, some for meditation, and so on. You cannot go in and out of meditation. It is the support of all activity. In the diversity of everyday life the background remains always the same and all activities are spontaneous expressions of this background. In meditation living is spontaneous. Life flows on without reference to a controlling centre, an ego. The I-image looks for survival in situations. It seeks security in repetition and acquired patterns of behaviour. It endeavours to make everything new and unknown into the known. As long as this controlling sense of individuality is functioning, we can never come to spontaneous living, to the non-state from which all states spring.

Meditation is the background of all doing, all activity. It is often taken to be a giving up of activity. But stopping the mind is not meditation. This very giving up is still an activity. Meditation is the stillness behind all activity and so-called non-activity.

Meditation is all-inclusive: all its expressions are within itself.

Q. You say we are meditation and to proceed to meditate is a going away from meditation. If it's not something I can do, how can I be beyond doing?

A. Simply be aware that you are almost always in doing, that you control, produce, judge, interpret. Take note, too, that when you try to avoid something it is still an activity and belongs to that very thing you are trying to avoid. There can be no transformation through trying. Meditation is not mind tranquillity. You can stop your thinking by discipline but it is not a free mind. As soon as you really see this you have stepped outside the process.

Q. Many traditions emphasise a systematic practice of meditation. Is there any value in this?

A. Meditation is not between 7.00 and 8.00 a.m. and 5.00 and 6.00 p.m. To learn something practical like a language or a musical instrument you need to practise. But you cannot practise what you are. One practises for a result in space and time but our fundamental nature is causeless and timeless. The moment you intend to meditate there is a subtle projection of energy and you identify with this projection.

When you become responsive to the solicitations of silence, you may be called to explore the invitation. This exploration is a kind of laboratory. You may sit and observe the coming and going of perceptions. You remain present to them but do not follow them. Following a thought is what maintains it. If you remain present without becoming an accomplice, agitation slows down through lack of fuel. In the absence of agitation you are taken by the resonance of stillness. It is like being alone in the desert. At first you listen to the absence of sounds and you call it silence. Then suddenly you may be taken by the presence of stillness where you are one with listening itself. This shift in perspective proves to you first-hand what hitherto you accepted second-hand as a possibility: that there is no meditator, that the idea of a meditator meditating is only a mind production, a figment of memory. This discovery is the point where the intellect comes to a standstill and you are seized by that silence which is the canvas for the whole palette of perception. At this point you will no longer feel the need to experiment in your laboratory. Tranquillity becomes more and more integrated into daily life.

Q. Is there then a place in daily life for sitting in meditation?
A. Our natural state is quietness but you know yourself only in doing, which hides the background of tranquillity. Take note of the desire to sit in meditation. Don't stop it, go away, avoid or control it. Look at it as you look at waves in the ocean. But be careful. You may think you are looking at the waves when looking is still an idea. In complete looking there is no psychological interference either as interpretation, emotivity or distancing. There is no introversion of the senses. They are still there as long as you have ears and eyes and a nose. If you aim to free yourself from the senses, from agitation, you are still projecting an outside, an other. It reinforces the subject-object relation.

When you are alert you will see that there are brief moments in your daily life when tranquillity appears. If you don't ignore this stillness but let it take you, it will increasingly solicit you and the desire will arise to be this stillness knowingly, that is, continuously. Thus meditation draws you to itself. You will come to see that although the mind may occasionally be still, its nature is movement, and that real tranquillity is the source of function and non-function alike.

Q. My life is so busy that I'm not even aware of these quiet moments you speak of. How then can I even begin to be taken by them?
A. It is important at first that you accept the possibility that your real nature is tranquillity, silence. You will then be open to a new perspective.

Begin to notice that the instant a desire is fulfilled there is a fleeting moment of desirelessness when no thought remains. This desire-free moment is of the same nature as the silence you continually are. It is a small window through which, if you look, light floods into your shadowy room. The same stillness appears in the space between two thoughts or when an action has been accomplished and there is nothing to be done immediately afterwards. This stillness is fulfilment.

In daily life there are moments when the thinking process comes naturally to a stop. But it is not an absence of producing. You feel yourself in completeness because there has been no will involved. Take note just before going to sleep when the body gives up being a body. It is like the setting sun. You watch the sun and feel yourself the seer. So if you watch your body dissolve in totality, there may come moments when you feel yourself still awake. In the morning when the body wakes up, it is like the rising sun. Let the body wake up slowly. Then you see that you are already awake before the body reappears. This awareness which is not associated with the body-mind is the same as that which is between thoughts and desires.

Q. When I follow the solicitations to be still and I sit quietly, I fall asleep. What can I do about it?
A. First, see that you are asleep in daily life, that your looking is mainly memory, that you don't inquire, don't really explore. Objects that are seen through memory become boring because memory is the already known. Take note of this. In reality every appearance is new but the I-image, which finds security in repetition, is the cause of anticipation in all your looking. When you really see a tree, all your being is engaged. You don't see only the leaves and branches; you feel survival in the tree, its dynamism, the desire to take light, maybe its suffering. The tree becomes an open secret which you find fascinating. If you are not awake in alertness, you will sleep with your projection.

Q. In the laboratory of meditation is there a good position for coming to a tranquil mind?
A. Be clear. No position can help or hinder being in stillness, but as body and mind are one, a relaxed body brings you to a quiet mind. Every position which is comfortable is the right position.

Q. What about techniques that use objects for meditation?
A. All technique aims to still the mind. But in fact it dulls the mind to fix it on an object. The mind loses its natural alertness and subtleness. It is no longer an open mind. Meditation is not meditating on something. Focusing on an object keeps you a prisoner in the known. Meditation belongs to the unknowable.

Stilling the mind by techniques can bring a certain relaxed state but the moment you leave it, the problem of daily life continues. The practice of regular meditation may make you familiar with a peaceful state which you remember in daily life. Apparently you live with less agitation, but this relaxation is still a state of which you are aware. It is a state of duality. Though it has therapeutic value it has nothing to do with our real quietness. For it still belongs to a function.

A still mind, a relaxed state, is an object of awareness, a fraction, and a fraction can never bring you to the whole. It may give you a glimpse of tranquillity but there is a great danger that if you proceed this way you will become fixed in the perception. For all progressive teachings, the transition from the subtle state of deep relaxation to the permanent non-state remains an enigma.

Q. When I sit quietly many thoughts and feelings come up. How shall I face these?
A. What comes up are residues of the past accumulated through day-dreaming. Remain present to them, free of all motive to suppress them. If the upcomings are referred to a centre they will be pushed into the unconscious or referred to the already known. The residues are given life by association of ideas.

All that comes up is conflict, created by the reflex to take oneself as a fraction, a separate entity. When there is no longer a centre of reference these conflicts come up like bubbles from the bottom of the ocean, and, meeting no obstacle at the surface, they disappear for ever in the empty space of your being present.

Elimination can never occur through analysis. It can only happen in your full awareness without the obstruction of the mind. Transmutation can only take place in Presence.

Q. Who is it that wants to meditate?
A. The point of sitting in meditation is only to find the meditator. The more you look, the more you will be convinced that he cannot be found.

First, inquire about your need to meditate. Where does this need really come from? From the desire to be fulfilled, to be in tranquillity. So the need to meditate comes from a feeling of lack. Make this lack an object of inquiry. What is it? A lack of wholeness. You take yourself for a meditator, an entity in space and time, and try to fill this isolation by meditating. But the meditator can only meditate on what he already knows and he himself belongs to the known. It is a vicious circle.

Fundamentally, you are nothing, but you are not aware of this and project energy in seeking what you are. It is a centrifugal movement taking you away from your home ground.

When, by self-inquiry, you find out that the meditator does not exist, all activity becomes pointless and you come to a state of non-attaining, an openness to the unknowable. There comes a stopping of the dynamism to produce and all the energy projected and dispersed in end-gaining is released and returns to its natural freedom without fixation or boundaries. You find yourself in a state in which all known points of reference have vanished.

Q. I have felt the need to go into silent retreat. Where does this urge come from?
A. From silence itself. Go deeply into the urge to be silent and not the mental interference of how, where and when. If you follow silence to its source you can be taken by it in a moment.

Q. I have a desire to go into silence for a long time because not speaking helps me see more clearly the agitation of the mind.

A. Silence is being free of producing. What is the need to give up speech for a few months? You will come no closer to understanding the nature of the mind and all existence through not speaking. The abstinence of voice production is not silence because thinking goes on in its usual agitated way. Many people in India indulge in not-speaking but the machine keeps running. We can only think through words. Thinking is subtle pronunciation where the sound is felt but not articulated, so there's no meaning in not speaking. Speech is beautiful. Our body is built out of speech. Every part, all matter, has its own sound, its own vibration.

A *brahmacharya* does not come to real silence by voluntarily giving up the natural functions of the body, but by taking note of all mechanical acting so that energy is not wasted. When you become familiar with listening, with observation, you begin to take your senses and thinking faculties as vehicles. The important thing is to come to know how you function. Voluntarily stopping the voice or thoughts is violence. It has absolutely nothing to do with real tranquillity.

Q. How do I bring my thoughts to quietness?
A. Not by forcing silence. See only that you fuel them by the mechanical reflex of the I-image. You live for the most part in association of ideas and interpretation. When you see this clearly you are no longer an accomplice and expended energy is diminished. Thinking becomes less concrete and what is left you'll feel as subtle energy, a kind of impulse. The energy localised in the impulse is no longer driven to strike the brain to find the symbol, the word. Even this impulse will eventually reduce itself

in your observing. Then there will be a sudden trans-ference of emphasis from the watching as perception to watching as being. The observed being fixed energy dissolves in observing, in energy without concentration. You have the impression that watching loses localisa-tion and you are expanding in a space without centre or periphery. In this emptiness, this non-state, all states appear and disappear.

The first thing is to become familiar with seeing and listening without interpretation. Stay away from the already known.

Q. What is one-pointedness?
A. Generally understood it is the same as concentra-tion. It is focusing on one point to the exclusion of other points. This is combined with looking for a result. A still mind is not a mind without thoughts. It is a mind without agitation. Silence is nowhere and in this non-localisation mind function appears.

Most of the time you are concentrated. There's always the reflex to find yourself somewhere. In concentration you take something from the perception for yourself. In real observation the inner need to localise doesn't arise. When you take nothing from the perception it dissolves in attention.

When you come into a room, let the objects see you. Don't take seeing to them. Then your looking will expand and be multidimensional. Be aware of how often you concentrate, that is, take patterns of seeing with you. Your looking is not fresh but habitual. When your functioning is not concentrated, energy is released and unfolds. You may be surprised at what appears.

Q. Is contemplation the same as meditation?
A. Deep inquiry leads to contemplation, or prayer.

Through dedicated contemplation we can attune to consciousness, the light which constitutes all phenomena. This light is our intrinsic nature. Our being is always shining. Our real nature is openness, listening, release, surrender without producing or will. Prayer or contemplation is welcoming free from projection and expectation. It is without demand and formulation. It invites the object to unfold in you and reveals your openness to you. Live with this opening, this vastness. Attune yourself to it. It is love. Ardent contemplation brings you to living meditation so ultimately they are one.

Q. From where does the desire come to be the silence knowingly?
A. The desire comes from what is desired. It is stillness attracted to itself in all its expressions. It is Love loving itself in the Beloved. There is nothing personal in this original desire.

Silence is the continuum in the three states of waking, dreaming and dreamless sleep. In deep sleep real quietness is reflected. When the body wakes up in the morning we say, 'I slept well.' Since the body was not present in our awareness, the saying doesn't refer to the body. It belongs to the deep quietness imprinted in us. In this way deep sleep awakens the longing for peace, for meditation, in all states.

Q. If one lives in this non-state you speak of, how does one function in the world?
A. Meditation, being the support of all activity, is not affected by any functions. Function is in space and time and is discontinuous. It is experience. Meditation is timeless and continuous; it is non-experience. In meditation there is no centre of reference and no repetition. It is a constant inner position of tranquillity. Action lives in this

tranquillity. Tranquillity is not affected by action or non-action. You can go through all the activities of your daily life without the background of quietness being affected. The background is not other than activity or non-activity, so it is pointless to give up one or the other to 'reach' the background. When you live in meditation, all flows out of the inherent intelligence of mind and body. You are no longer propelled by a conditioned centre. You are freed to be really creative. In living meditation the still light of creative intelligence illuminates all functioning and gives it true significance.

THE TEACHER AND THE TEACHING

When there's no teacher there's teaching
When there's no pupil there's understanding

Q. To actualise our potential it seems there's something to learn or understand.

A. We must distinguish between learning, accumulation of knowledge, and understanding or knowing, the immediate insight into our real nature. Appropriation of facts is necessary when studying a trade, an instrument, a language, and so on. But we cannot acquire what we fundamentally are. We can only recognise it. Recognition is an instantaneous happening.

Q. How can I come to this recognition?

A. In daily life there are glimpses of your primal knowing state. There are brief moments when you are in quietness without the dynamism of becoming. Generally, you overlook these moments because you tend to know yourself only in relation to situations, events and objects. When you acknowledge these moments of stillness, you become aware of a new dimension in your living, a dimension not related to any event or thought. Once you are open to this dimension it appears more often than you had ever noticed before.

Eventually you will see that what seemed to appear as moments is the continual background of all doing, thinking, feeling. It will envelop everything you do and think like an all-pervasive echo. It is this echo that brings you to look for the source of the echo, and to be ready for a guide on your journey.

Q. But don't most people look for a teacher long before the fore-feeling of autonomy brings them to it?
A. Then they are looking out of curiosity, hearsay or because it is fashionable. Or they want psychological support. You are only ripe for a teacher when you live in the fore-feeling. This intimation of your real nature is the inner guru.

Q. Do we need an external guru, a spiritual teacher, when we have an inner guru?
A. Theoretically no. Practically, yes, except in very exceptional cases. Logically, if we give ourselves totally to the fore-feeling we come automatically to what is fore-felt. But we are conditioned to take, not to let go. Attachment to our self-image hinders us from surrendering to our totality. It is the deep desire to be the fore-felt permanently which brings one to be ready for the outer guru.

Q. How can one look for a guru?
A. You cannot look for a teacher because you do not know what to look for. You cannot understand, cannot conceive of, a guide. You can only look for secondary functions, names, outer representations, magic, power, personality, etc. So you cannot try to find a teacher. All you can be is open to the teacher finding you.

Q. How can we know the false prophets from the seers?
A. In openness to the ultimate, free from looking for a physical teacher, you remain outside the psychological field and its projections and transferences. A teacher who takes himself or herself as a teacher needs those who

take themselves as disciples. In India and now in the United States there is a lot of guru-shopping and disciple-shopping. You will know when you have met the guru because he is not outside you and you become more and more independent. If you do not deeply feel your own autonomy you can be sure you are attached by projection and reaction.

Q. Would you say more about how we are found by the guru?
A. You are impelled by an inner urge which springs directly from the unknown. Questions come up: What is life? How to be free from anxiety? And so on. You come looking for answers and at a certain moment realise that the guru is not knowable objectively. At that moment the questions take on a life of their own. The answer is no longer sought from outside. To meet the guru is to lose your apparent self in your ultimate being. What we call the outer guru helps you by his or her pedagogy and presence to lose yourself. In finding yourself you are one with him or her and all living beings. The outer guru represents symbolically your real self. Once you have had the good fortune to hear that you are conscious-ness, the non-state, and that there is nothing you need to obtain or give up, don't make an object, an attitude of it. It should be as natural to you as knowing you are a man or a woman. The outer guru is only a pointer, so don't take him as anything else. One does not become attached to a signpost!

Many come looking for protection, authority, a mother, father, lover, doctor or therapist. Inquire deeply into why you come looking. You will see it arises from lack. You must face the lack directly and not escape into projections. A clear mind is also a peaceful mind and if the teacher does not bring you quickly to intellectual clarity, and greater autonomy, then go away. Do not stay, compelled by secondary factors.

Q. It seems that, paradoxically, the guru plays an important role in the direct path.
A. The guru is only a catalyst to the awakening in a new dimension. By the transparency of his presence he reminds you that the object cannot be emphasised. Thus he never encourages concretisation of his presence. Some sentimental transference may occur but since it cannot find a hold in him it eventually dissolves. In fact, the direct way is autonomous from the beginning. All energy that was expended in practices resolves in openness. Whereas in the progressive way the 'I' is subtly maintained through experiences, in the direct way no emphasis is put on experience. The real guru is nothing other than you. It is looking for you constantly, waiting for the moment of welcoming to appear. The so-called 'outer guru' is merely a transitional phase to show you that all projection is an illusion. Thus, the outer guru brings clarification when it comes from experience. If the outer guru is not completely transparent, free from the ego and the idea of being a guru, transferences will find a hold and you will become more dependent. If you do not feel yourself becoming autonomous, you can be certain you have not met your guru.

Q. What is a teacher?
A. When you become established in truth you may or may not be a teacher. To be a teacher takes a certain pedagogical gift, the capacity to pierce the mind directly so that the answer comes with the perfume of silence and unveils silence in the questioner. It is the capacity to see into the disciple and know instinctively in which way to present the teaching. There is no fixed teaching as

there is no fixed disciple. In fact there is no teacher, for the teacher is identical with what is taught. He is established knowingly in his teaching and it is at the core of his being that he knows there is nothing to teach.

One who lives in his real being takes himself for nothing. He brings the disciple to understand that there is nothing to teach. This creates a new perspective: that there is no disciple and no teacher.

The disciple takes himself for an ignorant person with something to acquire. When he meets the nothingness of the teacher and the teaching, he is brought to a letting go of his desire to be somebody who is enlightened, spiritual, religious, and so on. He is brought back to himself.

Behave as if you do not need any teaching, as if you are free, secure and contented. When you think there is something to acquire, you live in lack. The only thing to learn is how to approach.

Q. Is it only because of the language that you use 'he' for the teacher?
A. Oh absolutely! Language is often a problem because it comes mainly from the discriminating mind. The guru is impersonal, consciousness, neither male nor female. So it can manifest as either, or anything!

Q. You say there is nothing to obtain or do to know ourselves. That is clear. But isn't a certain vigilance needed to discover what we are not and couldn't it be called effort? Certain traditions say we are like harps that must be tuned before they are played.
A. Inquiry brings you to a well-orientated mind. The energy which is required comes from the right orientation itself. Inquiring is tuning your instrument. No effort is needed.

Q. What is the nature of the relationship if there is no disciple and no teacher?

A. All becoming is an illusion. To take oneself for something is a restriction. It is a fraction. All acts and thoughts coming from attraction are also fractional. One who lives in completeness cannot take himself as a fraction, a teacher. He is established in non-duality, sees only non-duality. He gives no hold to the so-called disciple to be something. Without the restrictions of personalities there is a meeting on mutual ground. In this meeting one knows exactly where he is but the other doesn't yet. Here there is a magic timeless moment and it may happen that the one candle that is alight will cause the other to catch fire. You cannot learn the truth, you must be caught by it.

Q. How does this transmission of light happen?

A. The flame is potentially there. When your beloved smiles at you there is a transmission of love beyond the physical gesture. In the oneness of love you smile in involuntary imitation.

Q. Is the disciple always aware of the transmission?

A. The so-called disciple is aware of moments of fullness with the so-called teacher, moments when there is emptiness of all personality, an empty openness. Then he is ready for receiving. The presence of the teacher is itself the transmission. There is no intention to transmit.

There may he moments when the disciple is freer than usual from all that he is not. The teacher may seize the opportunity.

Q. How is the transmission effected in the disciple?

A. Transmission is timeless but it can occur at any moment in time. The words of the guru are damp with presence.

When the words are heard but not fixed in the brain by memory or interpretation, their dampness remains. It is the dampness which keeps the word alive and at the same time annihilates its concreteness. This presence of the word is left as an echo of your own unknown presence. Truth is transmitted before the verbal answer. Expectation of an answer on the intellectual level hinders the answer from concluding in you. You can only really talk of an answer when it is felt in you. Authentic answers are first-hand. When the mind is cornered into a sincere 'I don't know', the living answer appears.

Q. How does my unknown presence become known?
A. The perfume of presence keeps the words of the guru alive as long as they need to be alive. This may be an instantaneous moment in time or many years. The word as an echo, an object-symbol, remains only to reveal its source, consciousness, the presence that you are in common with all things. In the moment of complete revealing, the actual words dissolve in their origin: stillness.

Q. Is the dissolution of the word a gradual process?
A. Let us be clear. It is not a progression. There is no evolution of presence. The dissolution of the word is bound to time but presence is merely covered by these formulations. When the words no longer find a hold, presence appears instantaneously, as the sun is always shining above the clouds.

Generally, conditioning is very strong. The tendency to keep all in the cage of the mind prevents the words of the guru from coming into their own. It may take many years for the intellect to loosen its grip. But the words of the guru have tremendous power. As the text says: Meditate on them.

Q. What does it mean exactly: Meditate on the sayings of the guru?
A. Live with them. The words are pregnant with their source. But their power can only be effective when they are not clouded by analysis, interpretation or mechanical repetition. You can never think about the words. You can only let them come alive in you. The words bring their own understanding. Let them act in you. Spontaneous transposition may take place on many levels. It is only through this spontaneous transposition into all areas of life that the word frees itself from itself, and you are suddenly awakened in your glory.

Q. Is it only through words and their dissolution that we come to an essential being?
A. There may be times when the disposition of the disciple is so open and mind-free that simply the presence of the guru stimulates the presence of the disciple. We call it transmission in silence.

Q. You say there is no teaching yet you talk about 'the words of the guru'.
A. Language, vocabulary, is a tool to bring intellectual understanding. Intellectual understanding and the letting-go of acquiring knowledge, attaining, becoming, must go together. All formulation is only to bring the intellect to see its limitations in dealing with what is unknowable in terms of percept and concept.

Of course different people come from different cultures and backgrounds, and the teacher, using different approaches, meets each according to his or her psychosomatic field. One can only teach what is teachable. What is teachable is the way. The truth and the light are not teachable. As the wind of wrong thinking covers the sun with clouds so only the wind of right thinking can uncover the sun. The truth and the light are our ever-lasting nature. In the end, therefore, there are no bad students, only bad teachers.

Q. You often say that we are not the doer but the witness of doing. This seems to be crucial in your pedagogy. Would you speak more about it?
A. When you say 'I have done this' or 'I am angry' you have established a personal relationship with the situation. When the situation does not refer to a centre, for example, when you think 'This is done; there is anger,' there is an absence of affective relationship. This absence feels like a space and the space around you frees you from attachment to the object. The object appears in this space. This feeling of space, the witness, is only a crutch, a pedagogical device, but it is a very important one. You can find the witness by seeing that whenever you take note of change your taking note is always in the present. To know the witness is to become acquainted with the observer of change. But this observer must not be an attitude. It is a dead-end to identify with a position. When the witness is not objectified it dissolves in the spaciousness which you are and to which it points. In other words, as long as there's an 'I' there's a witness, but when there's no 'I' there's no witness. The witness disappears with the person's disappearance.

Q. What do you think of traditional disciplines?
A. There are many traditional disciplines but these cannot be used in a systematic way. As a teacher one has all these forms at one's disposal. But all these techniques still keep alive the I-image. They keep you in the subject-object relationship. Real tradition occurs when the one you call a teacher is completely without image. He or she does not live in the restriction of being a 'teacher' with

something to teach, set ways of teaching, and disciplines. In his openness he brings you to freedom from your image. In this there is direct transmission; otherwise, you become stuck in forms and disciplines which can only lead to inflexibility and the blank state.

Q. But do you not feel that traditions carry the means to become free from tradition?
A. Let us be clear in our terminology. We might say that tradition is the transmission of Life. It is the essential, living experience of the fundamental non-state. Direct transmission needs no support. It is not bound by memory, time and space. All that is not direct transmission takes place in time and space. It involves memory. This we call 'traditional' and it includes rituals, doctrines, beliefs, myths, and so on. These ways of expression and teaching vary according to the individual culture and century. As long as the traditional is directly grounded in tradition it is a vehicle for transmission. In other words the timeless background must remain in all its expressions. When this is so, the traditional remains flexible, appropriate and timely. But when the traditional, the anecdotal, is emphasised, it loses its source in direct transmission and becomes inflexible. It cannot function for it has lost its original orientation, its true *raison d'être*, its life source. It becomes a shell without the animal in it.

Q. It seems that many people these days change traditions in the hope of finding truth.
A. It is a lack of insight to change one traditional frame for another. When you go deeply into your own religious tradition you will find the transcendental unity of all religions, the unity of the non-experience, the living understanding. Here there is no quarrel over dogma, ritual and mystical states, nor any place for comparison. It is

true that many of the traditional religions have become so identified with secondary factors that they give more hindrance than help in understanding. But if you inquire deeply as a Christian, Muslim, Buddhist, Jew, Hindu, and you understand it very profoundly, you come to the living truth. There are sages and saints in all religious traditions.

Q. I have met several spiritual teachers and always after some time I felt myself in the same state of dissatisfaction. Now, in listening to you, I see that I must meet a teacher without expectation, with an empty mind. Is this true?

A. Because you were accustomed to seeing objects, you were attracted by the personality of the teacher or the promise of some attainment. These belong purely to the body and stimulate certain feelings and chemical changes in you which remain as an echo for a while but in the end die away. When you are attracted on the personal level to a teacher, an idea, or an organisation, it feeds your patterns of emotivity and keeps you in the taking position. But there comes a time when the situation no longer stimulates you and there's nothing left to take, so you lose interest. Again, you feel bored with life and look around for new situations, new people, another addiction, a 'new' adventure. When you see that there is nothing remotely new in the latest attraction, that it is repetition, you will come to a standstill.

Q. My repeated disappointments have left me with a certain scepticism, a lassitude which prevents me from viewing things freshly.

A. Disappointment is a reaction in you which you superimpose on another. Scepticism and lassitude are psychic states just like excitement. See these things as facts in you, without wanting to change, add or subtract anything. When you face facts without wanting anything, you feel yourself in a dimension completely unknown to you. Then you are at the threshold of autonomy, what you really are, which has nothing to do with situations or feelings. There are many who live constantly in relation to other people, who need others to feel alive. The real teaching is to become autonomous and then to share the beauty.

Q. But one cannot live always alone. It belongs to biological survival to live with others.
A. Yes. But you don't need to be identified or attached to biology, the body. See that what you really are is autonomous, and then sharing has another significance.

Q. There was a time when I felt so eager in the spiritual quest and now I feel indifferent. What has happened to me?
A. Your inquiry was never strong enough. You emphasised the object too much. You were looking for states which eluded you or now bore you. Perhaps you looked for psychological support in the teacher and have now outgrown this need. Most people spend the whole of their lives going from one compensation to another, looking for various experiences, looking for a lover, a husband, a guru, money, etc. All this is enclosed in the mind and the person who thinks he wants these things is also in the cage of the mind. When you see that it is all a concept in the mind there's no more fuel and the mind becomes porous. It takes a certain maturity to see the cycle of lack, desire, compensation, boredom, etc. It takes readiness to see this and stop and ask 'Is this all there is to life?' Is there anything that is the support of all the changes, all the ups and downs and comings and goings?

Q. What might initiate these moments of stopping and asking such questions?

A. You might simply become bored with looking for compensation. This brings you to a recapitulation of your life. There are periods when we might find ourselves in an alley with no exit where energy is fixed. There are two main reactions to this situation. A more forceful character may feel the blockage of energy so strongly that he or she will take an action that shapes the rest of life, marrying indiscriminately, leaving the country, getting a divorce, having a child, etc. It is a desperate act, an escape that does not belong organically to that individual. It is a kind of explosion to try to get out of the cage. But of course it never takes you out and leads to a chain of such reactions. The less forceful personality may come to an absolute lassitude where there is not the slightest will to go out or even look for compensation. There is no more hope in anything and this brings about a kind of letting go. Then a small light may appear. The light is in you. It appears accidentally when you no longer focus on anything, not even the alley without exit. With the appearing of the light, energy is no longer crystallised. In both cases the result is the same: one comes, either through boredom or lassitude, to a giving up, a surrender. The absence of all hope is a gift.

Q. You seem to emphasise that understanding and experience should be concomitant. What happens if there is one without the other?

A. Understanding shows you all that you are not and brings about letting go. If the intellect is left behind there is a danger that too much emphasis will be put on feeling. Understanding reminds you that fundamentally what you are is not a state, an experience you enter and leave. A sage uses the world to go beyond it. He knows precisely the nature of function and he acts completely appropriately in the world. He is not of the world but is in it. Those we call 'mystics' put more emphasis on extra-mundane experiences than on being knowledge and its function in society.

Q. Is there a place for God in your teaching?
A. What you call God is a concept. You can add many qualifications, good, almighty, omniscient, etc., to this concept but it still remains intellectual and fuels a representation and a state of emotivity. To really know God you must free yourself from the idea of God. To come to experience God you must be empty of all personal images and projections which are false idols that take you away from being God. There is a saying, 'When you meet Buddha, kill him.' Meister Eckhart said that to meet God you must free yourself from the concept of God.

Q. Where does the desire to be united with God come from?
A. Union belongs to the mystic and oneness to the sage. The word union presupposes parts. You take yourself for a fraction, an isolated entity, and you long to return to what you suppose to be your origin. You may lose yourself in feeling, become identified with it in ecstasy. But feeling is still an affective state nourished by representation. When the ego is submerged in feeling it dies temporarily but returns in daily life. You can lose yourself temporarily in ecstatic states but when your real nature is not a state, why look for states?

Q. As language is dualistic, linear and sequential, therefore completely inappropriate to express the divine, wholeness, being, do we not need symbols?
A. Symbols are a necessary part of culture. They express

reality more deeply and suddenly than most words. The understanding of symbols does not belong to the everyday functioning of the mind. They pierce the mind and reflect its own ground in wholeness. Symbols take you beyond complementarity.

Q. Surely there is deep religious and idealistic longing that does not come from isolation?
A. Of course, ultimately it comes from the Self, your real nature. But longing needs information. The mind must be informed. When you accept that you are what you are looking for, the mind no longer projects an 'outside'. As long as you are looking outside yourself you suppose a separation. All effort automatically creates isolation. Explore with ease not by will and force. Let yourself be invited, be attracted. You say 'I am looking for truth.' But it is truth that looks for you.

Q. Can love alone, the *bhakti* path, bring you to realisation of your being?
A. Yes. But there comes a time when the *bhakta* sees that he lives in the world as well as in heaven. So he must come to understand life.

Very often in the *bhakti* path there is confusion. One is kept in the duality of admirer and admired. The mind must come to understand that what it most desires cannot be found 'outside', otherwise one remains like a dog sitting in front of a beautiful bone it can never eat.

Q. But cannot surrender to an all-encompassing love take one to love itself?
A. There is still a representation of somebody or something admired, loved.

Q. But the mind, the representation is consumed in love...

A. Yes, where there is really consummation of the person I agree. But mainly in this path there is attachment to the guru, the representation, the admired. Certain people feel a longing for they know not what, but they find a substitute, a definition for this unknown. It takes maturity to live in the yearning without concretising it.

Q. Are you saying that theoretically it is possible but practically it is a difficult path?
A. Yes. The real *bhakti* path is complete surrender. A surrender to one's own stillness. The emphasis is not on the object but on the surrendering. There may be a fore-feeling, an admiring state. Where it comes from the admirer does not know. When there is complete surrender to this admiring state then there comes a fusion of admirer and admired and what remains is only fullness.

Q. What is enlightenment?
A. The instantaneous insight that convinces you there is nothing and no one to enlighten.

Q. How can I come near to it?
A. Every step made to come near takes you away. 'It is nearer than picking a flower.' Be aware only of your unwillingness to give up wanting to produce. This intervention alienates us from the natural flow of life. Feel yourself in this awareness. Abide there and you will be taken by it. You will be in a new dimension, in an objectless expansiveness without reference. It is a moment of wonder, utterly without cause.

Q. It seems to me that we can experience only indirectly what is beyond body, senses and mind. How can we encounter it directly?
A. What and where is the underlying source of all our

perceptions? This discovery may be called the experience of enlightenment, though the light of perception is not on the film of experience. All religious, artistic, social or scientific visions that may occur are based on the known, accumulation, memory, and are only a prolongation of our real nature, timeless awareness. Our intrinsic nature is meditation, which is beginningless and endless. It is a non-state, a non-experience, and is self-sufficient, free from all need of stimulation and free from any motivation to build images and structures.

Q. What goes on in you when you hear a question and give an answer?
A. The question is heard in stillness and the answer comes out of stillness. They don't go through the mind, memory or a point of reference. We use words as symbols to point to understanding. As symbols they only have significance in the given moment. The answer comes out of silence. Receive it in silence. When you classify it, it loses the flavour of its source. Savour this taste and sooner or later it will attract you back to where it comes from, the living silence.

Q. Would you tell us about your experience of enlightenment?
A. If I told you now what could you do with the answer? When this question comes up, look immediately at the state you find yourself in. This question is an escape from facing the origin of the question. It comes out of curiosity, memory, hearsay, books.

Q. Was your awakening sudden or gradual?
A. The awakening is instantaneous but transmutation on the phenomenal level is in time.

Q. So a sage can mature after enlightenment?

A. One is struck on all levels but the transformation and harmonisation of the human substance, temperament, character and biological organism, are time-bound. Not all enlightened beings are teachers or become teachers immediately. The way to transmit truth may mature.

Q. What was your state of mind and body immediately preceding the awakening in consciousness?

A. Receptivity. It was absolutely non-orientated, non-localised, totally relaxed without projection, expectation or idea. Only in this completely relaxed state was I taken by grace.

Q. You said you saw flying birds at this moment. How did they strike you?

A. It seems to me that it was the first time that I saw facts without any interference on any level.

Q. So there was the seeing without intervention and then you were taken by the non-interference itself, is this so?

A. Yes. I was suddenly taken in being awareness, awareness without being aware of anything.

Q. At this point would you say in Zen terms that there were 'no mountains, no birds'?

A. Yes. The world ceases as illusion, as *maya.*

Q. But then you saw the birds again?

A. Yes. But they had no longer a separate existence. They appeared in my being, as an expression of myself.

Q. And did this new way of being remain with you?

A. Yes. It was not a manipulation of the intellect. Anybody can come to an intellectual representation of being, which may be very poetic.

Q. Is not this intellectual representation necessary, otherwise, experience remains accidental?
A. Intellectual clarity is important. It brings the mind to a giving up. If the mind is not informed it remains attracted by mental understanding which hinders it from letting go and being taken by understanding as total being.

Q. How did the different situations in your life appear after being established in this fullness?
A. Life went on as before but I no longer felt bound to existence. All activities were related to the wholeness that is being. Nothing felt accidental or unconscious. I would say all activities became sacred. As I was no longer bound to things and there was no localisation in form or concept, I felt the immensity, the vastness, in which all moved. All appeared in space. When you are bound to the activity you see only the activity itself and not as it stands in relation to the whole environment. When there is seeing from globality things appear in the situation that you have never seen before and there comes discernment and intelligent discrimination.

Q. Your behaviour changed?
A. Not by will. When one sees situations in their whole context without personal motivation, there is patience, and surrender, *gellasenheit* in German, that is not fatalistic. Change appears because you see the intrinsic value in things.

Q. If activity is no longer directed by personal will, is it not somehow directed by the character you bring into the world?

A. Yes, intrinsic character remains but it is purged from all that we generally call character which is reaction and resistance. This disappears, leaving only the 'natural' character.

Q. What if the character is, for example, ambitious, dominating, capricious, manipulating or violent?
A. There is the immediate reducing of the so-called personality to its basic characteristics. This brings a sudden rectification of the whole psycho-physiological structure. But it takes time to come to the complete harmonisation of energy.

Q. What does the character look like that is free of conditioning?
A. It has its own flavour, dependent on heredity.

Q. Are not most spiritual practices geared to improving character?
A. Many believe there is a somebody who needs improving.

Q. Can a sage still have likes and dislikes?
A. No. Like and dislike come from a centre of opinions. For the sage things are appropriate to the situation in the moment itself.

Q. But why does the action of various sages take such different expression?
A. Every situation brings its own action but the action is potential. The actualisation of the action belongs to the character, imagination, faculties of the body-mind. Similar situations can be furnished in different ways with out losing their intrinsic direction.

Some people express themselves in thinking, some in action, some in an artistic mode, some in silence. All expression comes out of giving. Ultimately it is all playing, an expression of universal energy. Certain sages are more in an earthly life than others. It belongs to their existence and all they bring to it. No way is better or worse than another. It is a completely mistaken idea, a wrong interpretation, that a wise human being leaves society. When a sage is in society but not of it he or she is the most positive element in the society.

Q. Why are there so few harmonious beings in the world?
A. The question is an escape from inquiring into your own lack of harmony. If I give you historical answers it will only reinforce your avoidance of a real question.

Q. Does a sage have any responsibility to teach and help others?
A. The word responsibility is not at all suitable. Teaching comes out of love, compassion, out of thankfulness. There is no sense of duty in it, no desire to personally improve the world. It is free from all motivation. It is a mistake to think the teacher does something. Transmission cannot happen intentionally. When there is ripeness the candle lights up. But there are those who escape being citizens of the earth. The task is to come to a balance, to be in the world but not of it.

Q. You say that if the teacher does not bring us quickly to intellectual clarity we must not remain, compelled by secondary factors like attraction to or dependence on the personality of the teacher. Also, there have been teachers who send people away when they see there has been no maturing. I have known you for ten years and although I feel a certain clarity on the psychosomatic level and can face my life more openly and even courageously, still I

WHO AM I?

do not feel there has been a great shift in the axis of my
life or that sudden awakening I long for. Why do you not
send me away?
A. There are different ways to teach. My way is to
approach someone at any level they may be at. If they
are sweeping rooms for a living then I help them to do
their work well. There is no yardstick to measure maturing because what you are cannot be objectified and compared. At each moment the past is consumed. Perhaps
you have not taken my sayings to heart. You have not
really lived with them. You have been more interested in
making money, learning the piano, having lovers, getting
married, your children. If you would give yourself to my
sayings as enthusiastically as you give yourself to other
things you would have what your heart deeply wants.
My sayings come from the heart.

Q. But I do feel I have taken your sayings seriously and
done all I can, yet I still feel no lasting freedom and
peace.
A. Go further. Really live with the sayings. Even dream
of them and you'll become attuned to them. You always
attain what you really want but you must really want it
with the heart. Remember, money and other desires do
not come from the heart, they come from the mind. All
desire comes from the deep desire for peace and freedom.
Live with the heart's deepest desire and it will bring you
to desirelessness.

Q. You talk of the absolute non-state as stillness. Others
describe it as love and peace. Is there love in your stillness?
A. In stillness there is an absolute absence of any state or
concept. You are this fullness. You cannot speak of love
and peace. This fullness is love, is peace, is happiness.

It is indescribable. Don't try to objectify love or peace and make a state of them. I see that you are still bound to affectivity. You want me to talk about love, to give you a hold, something to feel, to admire or obtain. I will not give you a straw to grasp, and in this emptiness you will be taken by yourself. You are love so don't try to be a lover.

Q. I feel many of my questions are irrelevant, how can I know what to ask you?
A. See where your questions come from. See that they emerge out of insecurity, agitation and fear. Take note that your formulation is an escape from facing these facts. Questions that don't come from the moment itself – questions that you look for – are not appropriate to these circumstances. The only appropriate questions are those that come up spontaneously from looking at the facts, your actual situation of doubt, agitation, insecurity jealousy, hate, greed, and so on.

You are accustomed to answers on the verbal plane and want me to give you such answers. But the answer to your real questions can never come on the verbal level. Real questions come out of the answer itself because facing the situation is the answer. So you can only find the answer in yourself. You are yourself the answer you are looking for in all questions.

Q. It's true. I came here expecting you to give me answers. How can I come to my own answer?
A. The real answer is felt within, not heard without. It lies in the open question. You will never be happy with second-hand answers, so why look for them? Live with your real question. Don't go away from it. In your opening to it, it unfolds in you. In your being open, you come to the living answer.

A CONVERSATION ON ART

Inquirer: For some time now I've been waiting to ask you both what you think art really is. Is it an amorphous collection of human expression or can we say more precisely what it is?

Philosopher: Ultimately all objects are pointers to truth and beauty but there are objects which, *par excellence*, bring us back to truth and beauty. These are works of art.

Inquirer: Does all that we generally call art have this power?

Philosopher: Art which strikes the senses and brings us beyond them to a timeless state could be called sacred art. Decorative or experimental art leaves us in the senses and in this sense can be called secular. Those great 'sacred' works which have the symbolic power to eject us into the impersonal realm are quite rare.

Inquirer: Let us talk about these works of art. What do you mean by saying they strike the senses and take us beyond them?

Artist: Is it not that aesthetic joy I sometimes feel when I am so taken by a work of art that it is no longer present as an object? There is only a feeling of wonder, delight and expansiveness where I forget space and time and am no longer in my senses, as you say.

Philosopher: Exactly. In aesthetic joy we come back to ourselves, close to our primal being. The delight of great works of art is that they have the power to point us to what we are, to that nakedness and playfulness of simply being, free from thought and self-consciousness.

Artist: Yes! When reading certain poems or listening to Beethoven's *Quartets* or when standing before certain sculptures by Henry Moore I am no longer in the everyday world but in a feeling of oneness and tranquillity. It is a feeling of being free from boundaries, from the routine of daily life and what I habitually call 'myself'. It is akin to those moments of wonderment I vaguely remember as a child.

Inquirer: Do you remain in this feeling or do you come back to the object?

Artist: I go back to the details to see what it is that delights me. The coming back is spontaneous, it is the desire to make the work my own. I explore the composition, recreate it point by point until there is nothing left to observe and then again I let myself be taken by joy without the presence of the object.

Philosopher: Yes. One returns involuntarily to explore a work because the senses are not yet completely integrated into the whole, the feeling of oneness, and are full of desire to be so. When we explore the details of a work point by point, the global feeling remains as the background and each detail is spontaneously referred to it. Attention thus remains expanded and in it the senses lose their objectivity and unfold. This time, however, they are integrated consciously in our awareness, so there is no immediate desire to come back to the details, the object part. That would be a reduction of the feeling of oneness. It is the marriage in gratitude of admiration and appreciation.

Inquirer: But eventually we long to hear or see the event again. Why is that?

Artist: When the senses are so exalted and transformed it is normal to want to be delighted again. We are creatures of the senses and aesthetic joy is the sensation of the gods. Great works of art are a source of inexhaustible delight.

Inquirer: Could we say that aesthetic fullness is fuller after the integration of the senses?

Philosopher: Fullness is then more grounded in the wholeness of life. Without the integration of all the elements, the feeling of oneness remains nebulous like a mystical experience. It is important that body and mind are integrated, that objective knowledge is not denied but incorporated in the wholeness of knowing as being.

Inquirer: You said that the object is full of desire to be integrated into oneness. What attracts the object?

Philosopher: We could say, like Plotinus, that it is an emanation of God and a return to God. Or we could simply say that the object is drawn towards its home ground, wholeness. In multidimensional attention where the senses are released the object loses its rigidity and unfolds in you, an unfolding that your mental interference hinders. At a certain point the last residue of objectivity is suddenly absorbed into the magnet of global awareness.

Inquirer: What exactly is it about these works of art that gives them the power to eject us into timelessness?

Artist: It is the perfect composition and balance of colour, form and sound which reveal the fundamental elements, light, space and silence; in short, the work must be harmonious.

Inquirer: Could we say that the harmony of the work echoes in us reminding us of our own harmony and this remembrance is the feeling of wonder you spoke of?

Wholeness is thus common to the work and the observer; otherwise, how could we be reminded of it so strongly?

Philosopher: Yes indeed. The fundamental elements are common to all. Art is a reflection of the harmony we are in common with all things. It contains globality within itself. Nature is harmonious and the human being is part of nature.

Inquirer: When we use the word 'harmony' what do we mean exactly? It cannot be anything to do with symmetry since nature is anything but symmetrical.

Philosopher: Harmony is the whole wherein everything exists without conflict. It is the same as beauty. Our real nature and the real nature of the work of art are one and the same. The work of art is a manifestation, a hint if you like, of this oneness.

Inquirer: So when we call a work beautiful it is because it reminds us of, and points to, our own beauty. Is beauty then subjective in some sense?

Philosopher: Not at all. In wholeness there is no subject or object, so how can there be subjectivity or objectivity? Beauty is one though its expressions are many. In beauty there is no object so how can there be a subject?

Inquirer: Though beauty is not relative or comparable because it does not lie in the so-called object, we could still say that certain works *inspire* beauty by their own beauty. But when we look at the variety of things that inspire our wholeness, our godliness, it is difficult to see any thread running through them at all. Our artist said that it was the composition which revealed the fundamental elements but this does not really help me. What more precisely about certain objects gives them their symbolic power to point beyond the senses to our real nature?

Artist: The composition is such that it sets free beauty and harmony. It does not emphasise the objective or material part so that you are not held in the anecdotal but are taken straightaway by the fundamental elements to which the composition points. Great works by different techniques call you to the spatial, timeless dimension. Volume is conceived in such a way that it liberates space, colour liberates light, sound liberates silence.

Inquirer: Are these fundamental elements our real nature?

Philosopher: They are the nearest manifestation of being. They are pure existence, its base, in contrast to the projected existence we take for granted. They have nothing to do with a point of view. When you are brought back to pure existence in light, silence and space, you are in the nearness of being which is the background of all manifestation and out of which all existence comes.

Artist: Great works of art bring us a taste of what we are. I feel my own weightlessness in the columns and capitals of ancient Greek temples, for example. They are so perfectly proportioned that they are at home in heaven and on earth and they leave me nowhere! And when I am in a Romanesque or Norman church I am brought back to my centre by the simple, pure lines. They inspire inner tranquillity. One is reminded of one's own light and spaciousness in some sculptures by Brancusi or Arp or Henry Moore, or in Chinese paintings of the sixteenth and seventeenth centuries. And you have only to listen to Bach's *Art of the Fugue* or Beethoven's *Quartets*, as I said before, to be taken by silence. The real music is between the sounds and lingers long afterwards, the way a beautiful poem lives as an echo long after the reading, or a lovely human being lives in you long after the meeting. That is why, after a beautiful concert, I cannot under-

181

stand why people make such a barbaric noise before the last notes have unfolded and dissolved in our silence. I remember some lines of Walt Whitman:

> *All music is what wakes in you when you are reminded of it by the instruments*
>
> *It is not in the violins and the cornets ... nor the score of the baritone singer*
>
> *It is nearer and further away*

Philosopher: It is clear that you have really felt what is the essence of our conversation. Great art awakens us to ourselves. True admiring is behind all emotivity and true art is not interested in stirring sentiments.

Artist: Ah! But an emotion comes up that has nothing to do with everyday emotivity, our usual repetitive emotional states. Each time it is new, an expression of profound gratitude from the deepest regions of our being.

Inquirer: So if I understand correctly, the symbolic power of a great work of art arises when the artist does not emphasise the anecdotal elements. Could we explore this artistic economy?

Philosopher: Where there is no psychological intervention, when the person of the artist is absent there is no temptation to over-express and spontaneously there is economy, as you say. This is the artist as ascetic. The artist who is selfless knows instinctively what to put but even more what not to put. Beautiful art is not whimsical. It does not bind you to the form and content. It is so construed as to lose its concreteness. The weightlessness of Greek and Egyptian architecture is due to space and form coming together. Where two lines meet and reduce in oneness is the point where opposites have no more hold. In this absence of conflict, the spectator is open to harmony and is taken by joy without representation, his own harmony.

Artist: That is why art must make a spring appearance. It must be a hint. It is partially secret and this secretness is sacred. The creative power of great works of art is the revealing of the sacred. That is our real nature.

Inquirer: Has the artist a feeling of the sacred function of his work?

Artist: Oh yes, though he does not name it. In the artist is an original feeling of fullness which spills over into thankfulness. This in turn moves into the desire to offer or share. The artist lives with the burning desire to share the original feeling. It is the background to his or her life. This offering looks for expression. It looks to become specific. One doesn't need to be a great artist to feel this. It belongs to all human beings. But in the artist, because of his capacities, there is, at a certain moment, a condensation of energy. The desire becomes more localised. The artist struggles to express it, to find the appropriate representation, to make it concrete in its highest form. This concretisation is the extinction of desire, the accomplishment of offering. The moment the representation is given there's a relaxation of energy.

Inquirer: You said the representation, the artistic vision, was given. Does this mean there is no thinking in the creative process?

Philosopher: Creative insight has nothing to do with thinking. Of course one uses rational thinking, the already known, to put it in space and time, but this thinking is grounded continually in the global insight.

Artist: An artist is only a receiver. He knows that if he is a producer he will only produce from memory. The artist must thus lay himself bare to inspiration. His own well is very shallow. He must tap into the global source of creativity. Inspiration always comes as a gift, suddenly, from the deepest layers of being, which are completely impersonal. All great artists know that in one way or another they are only channels. Bach was very aware of this.

Inquirer: How does the artist lay himself open to inspiration?

Artist: In the same way as any seeker. He is steeped in his medium with a longing, an earnest desire, to come closer to its creative source. When a painter sees a flower he does not see it in isolation but in relation to other things, to space, light and colour. It is the same with any artist. Everything is transposed in the medium. At the same time the artist knows he can do nothing without inspiration and that inspiration cannot be invented, so the artist as artist, as doer, thinker, intender, abdicates. He is an artist in waiting. He lives in receptivity, in welcoming, in his medium, but he has no idea of what will come. There is no avidity or anticipation in his eagerness. Sometimes he may have a theme but he lives in openness as to how it will appear to him. He gives himself to empty receptivity and suddenly, unexpectedly, is absorbed in the global vision of a work. This timeless moment of oneness is the beauty of the artist himself seen through the window of his medium. He is struck in awe and wonder. He has a feeling of fulfilment and oneness with all things and out of this deep gratitude comes the urge to offer. It is a sacred emotion free from all personal feeling. The subject matter is only a pretext to express this offering in space and time.

Inquirer: So the work itself is not important to the artist?

Artist: The medium is only a channel to come to the creative source and to reveal it. What makes a great artist is his ability to surrender his personality. Great art has nothing to say, has no purpose, no intention. It is a free gift. Its meaning lies in its purposelessness.

Inquirer: Are any details seen in that flash when beauty is transposed in the global vision of the work?

Philosopher: No. The work is not seen with the ordinary mind's eye which functions in sequence. It is seen by the eye that opens when the mind is free of all expectation, in moments of deep relaxation away from the contraction of habits of thinking. This may happen to any of us in intervals during the day when the I-image is absent, or between deep sleep and waking before the brain begins its sequential functioning. We have it in certain dreams, called *songes* in French, where in an instant we see a whole situation that we later draw out into time and describe as the 'future' or the 'past'.

Artist: Do you remember Van Gogh's reply when his brother Theo asked him how he came to interpret trees as flames? He said that several times he saw the four seasons in one moment. And Mozart wrote that he heard many of his works in a single instant.

Inquirer: Does this global vision remain during the execution?

Artist: Yes. The artist lives with the initial vision and the feeling of offering, the thankfulness, inspires the execution at every moment. This is the artist on fire who cannot sleep until he has expressed his insight. The execution may, however, cause an artist great suffering because he fears he cannot do justice to the tremendous vision. Sometimes he may lose the deep feeling that motivates him and compensate with ideas or technique. When you are observant you can feel this in the work.

185

Inquirer: You said that the artist suffers when he cannot express his vision. There is a commonly accepted view that suffering also inspires an artist, but since his personality is absent at the moment of creativity this cannot be true, can it?

Philosopher: Not at all! I am tempted to say it is a bourgeois view to assuage feelings of guilt but we won't go into that! In any case it is an opinion based on superficial observation. No real art arises out of emotivity and so-called artists who look for artificial stimulation in suffering never come to the creative source. They are bound to the stimulation. Suffering is a powerful emotional state, but at the creative moment it is objectified and becomes a pointer to freedom from suffering. It is this freedom that is the home ground of all creativity. What can cause great suffering is, as our artist said, the isolation from this freedom and the desire to come back to it through the execution. Ideas are not emphasised in art but one could say that the representation of harmony, what the artist understands by perfection, is an ideal. This ideal could be called the 'muse' but it is not a cultural acquisition. It belongs to deep aesthetic feeling. To be able to represent this ideal depends on the craftsmanship. The artist knows that he can never completely exteriorise his vision. He can only approximate it. This may create suffering but it is not the idea of suffering commonly accepted.

Artist: I entirely agree and might add that the artist, unlike the ardent truth-seeker, often sees the divine only through his medium and not his whole life. Through his medium he has a window to beauty. But he might only have the one window so he is lured to it, to be an artist. In a way he does not see his own beauty because he objectifies it into the beauty of the work of art. This separation causes conflict, and the longing to resolve the conflict drives him back to the studio.

Inquirer: Is pleasure equally a pointer for the artist?

Philosopher: Yes. Absolutely. But generally when one is in pleasure one is completely and contentedly involved in it. Suffering is more antagonistic than pleasure. It is less harmonious. The desire to free oneself from suffering is greater than the desire to free oneself from pleasure. In freeing oneself from the object one is ejected into autonomy. In this space the inspiration occurs.

Inquirer: You say the artist suffers because he cannot do justice to the feeling of globality, the vision of the work. What is the reason for this inability?

Artist: You cannot express yourself without the tools of expression. There is a point when the inner feeling is so great that one is urged to expand one's repertoire of technique in order to express the feeling in space and time. In a sense, the magnitude of the feeling of offering and technique go together just as intellect and experience are concomitant in the truth-seeker. Technique is a means to an end. Yet it vanishes completely in the work of art.

Inquirer: We said that harmony is the whole wherein everything exists without conflict, and that it is manifested in different ways. The artist intuitively recognises certain archetypes of form, original manifestations, and must be gifted to transpose these into the creative work. According to the ancient Greeks the archetypes of form are expressed by laws which are learned. Do you agree or can it be intuitive knowledge?

Artist: Nature is free symmetry where there are no right angles. The form of a leaf, a petal, a wave, the movement of bones, can be put in a geometrical structure but because there is no repetition in nature and it is thus beyond comparison and in this sense perfect, there can he no imitation. The creative artist does not copy nature but transposes one perfection into another. Certain art forms call for a greater knowledge of the geometrical structure. But this learning is more in the nature of remembering than acquisition. Knowing rules is not enough. Inspiration comes when the rules are laid aside. It is paradoxical. To be inspired you must forget yourself and all you know, and to execute the inspiration you must leave yourself forgotten but come back to the known craftsmanship. The artist must be completely flexible.

Inquirer: What is the relationship between function and beauty?

Philosopher: Everything is in beauty. Function is in beauty and the laws of harmony and composition are in beauty. Beauty, remember, is that in which there is no conflict, so all the elements of the art must be taken into account. There is a story in the *Jataka* where the Bodhisattva employs a master architect to build a great hall to suit their purposes in every way. The architect cannot grasp what the Bodhisattva means by 'suitable' and says he can only work in the tradition of his craft. The Bodhisattva then lays out a plan himself, determining the form entirely by the use to which it will be put. It is not a piece of self-expression. The Bodhisattva simply knows better than the architect all that is in the mind of the All-Maker.

Inquirer: So for the Bodhisattva the 'function' of the hail included many things the architect could not see because he was limited by a particular idea. It is a pity today that most architects have reduced function to economics, self-expression and experimentation and have forgotten the harmony and beauty that is the ground of their existence!

Artist: Yet the buildings we live in determine how society functions. Many people feel agitated and are not aware that the room they are in is not the right proportion for them, or is too dark, and so on. We have become so passive in our observation!

Inquirer: How can we become active observers and admirers again?

Philosopher: Turn your whole being to the object, not simply the mind with the eyes or ears. Like the artist you are only a receiver. An audience must not interpret or come to a speedy conclusion. When you look at a beautiful sculpture and immediately say to yourself, 'It reminds me of ...' you make it a mental representation and cannot feel the beauty unfold in you. But do not remain passive. Let the work invite your participation. Aesthetic joy is the feeling of being awakened in creative participation, when you see the work globally as the artist first saw it. Through collaboration, the artist, work and audience come together in oneness. The vision comes as a surprise offering, a gift, to the artist but it is only unwrapped in the observer.

Inquirer: Could you say that art is fundamentally social if it comes to completion in the receiver?

Philosopher: In this sense, yes. It is the inherent function of the artist to take us beyond the common sense of daily life and to bring beings together in oneness. A great work of art belongs to nobody. In great artists there is no feeling of satisfaction and achievement which is the person taking credit for his own creation. It remains sacred, a symbol, an offering from God and an offering back to God. The artist feels himself only as the instrument of manifestation. Because the artist is completely focused on the execution, when the work is finished there may be a feeling of liberation.

Artist: The creative collaboration is always subconsciously present in the artist during the execution. His deep feeling of oneness and sharing this with others is part of the wholeness of the vision. It tells him when to stop explaining his vision so that the other can take it up. Mark Rothko was aware of this. Great art never dominates with mental or sensual stimulation. It is not a drug for the senses like most art production we see. No work of art should state its concreteness to the extent that it gives no room for movement. There must be space for creative interaction to occur. Many people enjoy the paintings of very young children which are often spontaneous without mental intervention. In this freedom one feels free.

Philosopher: Anything that does not awaken our natural alertness is not a work of art. Productions that come from experimentation or psychological states are fractional and leave us in fraction. The talent of the artist lies in making the object objectless.

Inquirer: Does this mean that whatever awakens our alertness is a work of art? In other words, a work of art is not always made, it can be found?

Philosopher: It is always found in that it is always received. Art objects are symbols and point to wholeness but the work of art needs workmanship. It is a transposition and must be executed or built up in some way.

Inquirer: Is the artistic imagination, that is, the organ of the transposition, an intellectual process or does it occur spontaneously?

Artist: Imagination cannot be thought. It comes up when the personality is absent. It reveals what is hidden in nature. What appears in this openness depends on the fantasy and taste of the artist. Imagination comes up from the well of beauty and limitless expression and takes shape in the uniqueness of the artist's existence.

Inquirer: How does the artist know what is really creative imagination and what is a kind of elimination?

Philosopher: When you become more familiar with yourself, the distinction between what is true imagination and what is mental jugglery will become clear. Imagination arises from wholeness and leaves a global feeling. There is no personal involvement. One finds this impersonal spaciousness in *haiku*, which is a simple statement of facts that resolves in the presence of the reader. Often day-dreaming is called imagination. But day-dreaming always refers to an 'I' and involves aspiration. It is really only psychological survival. Of course dreams of becoming begin at a very early age and society encourages aspirations but day-dreaming keeps us in the process of becoming and prevents us from drawing from the creative source of being.

Artist: Couldn't we say that day-dreaming is simile and real imagination is metaphor? For example, if I say, 'Be like a bird in that tree,' you will remain here and visualise yourself there in the tree. However, if I say, 'You are a bird in that tree,' and you grasp this completely, there is total transposition and no room for comparison. You are the bird and your whole structure feels the wind, the movement of the branches and the smell of the leaves. You no longer picture yourself there. You are simply there. How different dancing, music, acting, painting would be in the two cases!

Philosopher: Exactly. The first is a mental process and therefore fractional. It involves duality. In the second there is no fraction. True imagination is not visualisation. One cannot be here and there at the same moment because consciousness is always one with its object. In visualisation there is always a quick succession of thoughts. In actually being the bird, the part, the music, there is oneness. Then all writing, painting, dancing, acting is transformed.

Inquirer: So when the senses are transposed in their wholeness nothing personal remains?

Artist: There is no one left who dances. 'How can we tell the dancer from the dance?'

Philosopher: But let us not forget that the artist does not get lost in his feeling. He is one with the action but knows himself in the acting. The 'himself' he knows is not the personality of the actor but what is behind the actor *and* the role he plays.

Artist: Of course the actor does not *act* Hamlet. That means two are on stage, the actor and his view of Hamlet. Only when the actor as doer is absent can Hamlet be present.

Philosopher: Hamlet is in him but he is not in Hamlet. He cannot he involved, lost in Hamlet, because 'he' is absent. The real nature of action is non-action.

Inquirer: I confess I have lost your meaning

Artist: When the actor goes on stage he does not take his usual collection of self-images, his personality, with him. He is empty of all memory, anticipation and so on. Through his preparation of the part, Hamlet has become an accumulation of experience just like any other part of his personality. And, like all facets of his personality, it appears in the moment and disappears into emptiness when not needed. The actor is penetrated in the moment itself. A part is reborn with each performance just as every situation calls for a new-born personality to appear. One does not wear the personality permanently nor repeat a performance in any situation in life. Everything that happens is new, fresh, unforeseen.

Inquirer: How then are we to approach traditional art in this feeling of timelessness and freedom from patterns?

Artist: Art may belong to the conventions of a century but the principles are timeless. Henry Moore, for example, uses the object scientifically to point to space. In traditional art the anecdotal is not emphasised either but is used to point to a collective meaning. One must, of course, be fully cognisant of the symbolic meaning to appreciate a traditional work of art. The form is only a pretext. The symbol takes us beyond the image. All religious art functions in this way. If you look at the sculptures of the Chola period in India with no comprehension of their meaning, you will be bound to the pretext, the anecdotal. You might admire but you cannot appreciate.

Inquirer: Is there not a distinction between pure aesthetic experience when one is taken beyond all feeling and the religious feeling that is inspired by some beautiful traditional works?

Philosopher: It is true. In both cases you are lifted from the personal realm. However, a religious work points to the cultural representation. Generally it evokes collective sentiments. Completely non-representational art may on the other hand free one from all representational connotations whatsoever. It can bring you to emptiness and light. However, if one already knows light and space, non-representational being, then a beautiful religious image could indeed bring you back to joy without object. The object is a mirror which reflects what you bring to it.

Inquirer: Is this not the essence of all symbolism, ritual and myth? When the personal or relative element is absent the transposition can he appropriated, or made one's own, at all times. What began as dependent on circumstances is now made impersonal and autonomous.

Philosopher: Of course it is a long subject for another day of conversation but I agree with you. What is released from arbitrary time and space and is made impersonal and timeless can he reborn over and over again in time. It is given universal freedom to be creative, that is, to reawaken its original cause, the exaltation of the senses. Specific, localised time is made timeless so that it can again come back to time and space but with the full bloom of the universal and collective.

Inquirer: This movement of creative events is a recognition and expression of the fact that we are all links in the chain of being, microcosms of the macrocosm. Works of art, ritual and myth are an affirmation and exultation of our fundamental oneness. But coming back to art, would you say that art which is free from representation is a higher art form?

Philosopher: Let us be clear. Art that is free from the object is not abstract. Abstract, non-figurative art is generally intellectual, what I call 'decorative'. It does not utilise the global body sensations, but is born from idea. As such it can only unfold in fragments of the body. At best it acts as a palliative, but it can never take you beyond fraction.

Inquirer: So in the coming together of admiring and appreciation the whole body comes into play?

Philosopher: It is important to realise the subtlety of the body, to be sensitive enough to know when beauty is revealed in us and when it is not. All harmony is in us.

We are a microcosm of universal harmony, thus we must listen to the echo in us. When we hear music or see a painting or are in a building we must take note of how it acts in us, how we react in mind, body and sentiment.

Inquirer: I have heard that music, for example, strikes us in three regions, the lower (sexual), middle (abdominal), and upper (cerebral), corresponding to rhythm, melody and harmonics. African and contemporary music often emphasise rhythm and Bach stressed harmonics.

Philosopher: Yes. We must be aware of how we are affected and not identify with a fraction. True appreciation is not conditioned by ideas. Since we are all made of the same fundamental elements, great works of art and nature have universal appeal in any century. The alchemical transformation when observer and observed become one is not bound to time and place.

Inquirer: It is clear that it is important to learn, not what to look at, listen to and so on, but *how* to look and listen. Yet how can I be alert taking note of sounds, how they act in me and how I react to them, and at the same time be passive, remaining in the global background, the silence out of which all things come?

Philosopher: One must explore as a child explores, in openness. It is only possible when the controller, the ego, the propagator of views is absent. Listening is then not fixed in the ears, nor looking in the eyes nor tasting in the mouth. So don't listen to a sound, let it listen to you. Don't look at this flower, let it look at you. The moment you are receptive, all the senses are enhanced. When there is no fixation on one sense faculty then all can come into play. One sense is merely a channel for the rest. Allowing the transposition from one sense to the exaltation of all is a way of living with objects.

Artist: This is what happens when I see the colour red and feel it as warm, passionate or aggressive. Sometimes it even has a certain smell! Blue produces in me a sensation of quietness, space and coolness. And we talk of sounds that are round or flat or sharp.

Inquirer: If this transposition is successive how can I come to that global joy where all the senses are integrated in the whole?

Philosopher: When there is no fixation, no concentration or direction, the senses relax their grasping quality, their hold on the spontaneous unfolding of all the body. Alertness without focus invites the object to tell its story. Welcoming is attractive and when objects are released from fixation by the senses they are spontaneously attracted into welcoming as to a magnet. At a certain point there is a sudden movement and the residues of fixed energy, residues of perceptions, are integrated in global awareness. There is a complete reorchestration of energy.

Inquirer: Is this what happens when the sight of flying birds or the sound of water may suddenly be a door to global awareness?

Philosopher: Yes, when there is the ripeness that comes in welcoming. As the artist lives constantly in his medium knowing it is the door to the source of creativity, so the truth-seeker lives in the medium of his real nature, welcoming, openness, at every moment. When you live as the body, all appears as body; when you live as mind, all appears as mind; when you live as an artist, all appears as colour, sound, space and form; when you live as a scientist, all appears as relation; when you live in consciousness, all appears as consciousness.

Inquirer: So the artist lives in feeling and its expression and it is inherent in the artist to share this with others.

The scientist objectifies his knowledge; he says, 'I know.' But the truth-seeker does not emphasise feeling or knowledge or any object, but knowing as being, so after the intuition of being he no longer has the reflex to objectify and remains in oneness. Thus he is in continual offering.

Artist: Is not the creative desire as close as we can come to understanding Cosmic Desire out of which all creation comes? Surely the process of creation in the artist is the same as in the creation of the universe with the difference that cosmic desire never comes to complete exhaustion because its concretisation is infinite? This desire remains without beginning and end. It is the archetypal desire. God's activity comes to rest only in knowing as being, where stillness meets itself. The transparency of the sage allows being to meet itself. Fire extinguishes fire.

Inquirer: After all this can we say that wisdom and love of art go hand in hand?

Philosopher: It is certain that wise men and women love beauty, because it echoes their own beauty. Sages are versed in the art of living and execute their offering through their being and teaching. Real sages, like great artists, are rare. Their whole living is an offering in which the listener is invited to participate. Like the artist at the creative moment, the sage is ego-free, simply a channel, and like the artist the wise one allows those who come looking for truth to find accomplishment in themselves.

Artist: And yet at the moment of looking at, or listening to, a beautiful work of art are we not all sages? In that instant where are we three? Where even is the feeling of togetherness or sharing? There is only looking, only listening. There is only oneness, silent communion in being. Is this not the essence of wisdom?

197

Inquirer: I will live for a long time with the feeling of this conversation. Existence is the work of art in which all come together in a festival of love!